T0313310

AGILE AUDIT TRANSFORMATION AND BEYOND

Security, Audit and Leadership Series

Series Editor: Dan Swanson, Dan Swanson and Associates, Ltd., Winnipeg, Manitoba, Canada.

The Security, Audit and Leadership Series publishes leading-edge books on critical subjects facing security and audit executives as well as business leaders. Key topics addressed include Leadership, Cybersecurity, Security Leadership, Privacy, Strategic Risk Management, Auditing IT, Audit Management and Leadership

Information System Audit: How to Control the Digital Disruption
Philippe Peret

The Security Hippie
Barak Engel

Finding Your Granite: My Four Cornerstones of Personal Leadership
Douglas P. Pflug

Strong Security Governance through Integration and Automation: A Practical Guide to Building an Integrated GRC Framework for Your Organization
Priti Sikdar

Say What!? Communicate with Tact and Impact: What to say to get results at any point in an audit
Ann M. Butera

Auditing Information and Cyber Security Governance: A Controls-Based Approach
Robert E. Davis

The Security Leader's Communication Playbook: Bridging the Gap between Security and the Business
Jeffrey W. Brown

Modern Management and Leadership: Best Practice Essentials with CISO/CSO Applications
Mark Tarallo

Rising from the Mailroom to the Boardroom: Unique Insights for Governance, Risk, Compliance and Audit Leaders
Bruce Turner

Operational Auditing: Principles and Techniques for a Changing World (Second Edition)
Hernan Murdock

CyRM^{SM}: Mastering the Management of Cybersecurity
David X Martin

For more information about this series, please visit: https://www.routledge.com/Internal-Audit-and-IT-Audit/book-series/CRCINTAUDITA

AGILE AUDIT TRANSFORMATION AND BEYOND

Toby DeRoche,
MBA, CIA, CCSA, CRMA,
CICA, CFE, SA, cAAP

CRC Press
Taylor & Francis Group
Boca Raton London New York

CRC Press is an imprint of the
Taylor & Francis Group, an **informa** business

First edition published 2022

by CRC Press
6000 Broken Sound Parkway NW, Suite 300, Boca Raton, FL 33487-2742

and by CRC Press
4 Park Square, Milton Park, Abingdon, Oxon, OX14 4RN

CRC Press is an imprint of Taylor & Francis Group, LLC

ISBN: 978-1-032-06289-1 (hbk)
ISBN: 978-1-032-06290-7 (pbk)
ISBN: 978-1-003-20157-1 (ebk)

DOI: 10.1201/9781003201571

Typeset in Adobe Caslon Pro
by KnowledgeWorks Global Ltd.

"Intelligence is the ability to adapt to change."

Stephen Hawking

Contents

1

DEFINING AGILE AUDIT

What Is Agile Auditing?

As more audit departments are exploring agile audit, the definition of agile audit is becoming more apparent. Software developers and project managers often use agile to describe a mindset for producing results more quickly based on changing requirements and shifting priorities. For our purposes, agile auditing is a customer-centric approach to developing and executing audits, based on a shorter audit lifecycle from assessment to reporting, which focuses on gaining and sharing insights with management related to the most urgent risks in an organization. We can apply an agile approach throughout the audit lifecycle, encompassing the risk assessment, audit plan, fieldwork, and reporting phases. Throughout this book, we will use this definition to consider how an agile transformation can reshape the audit department.

To fully grasp the concept of agile auditing, it helps to start with the concept's origin. In the past 40 years, there has been a push to run business operations more efficiently through concepts like "just in time," "six sigma," "total quality management," and "lean." In early 2001, a group of IT professionals drafted what is now known as the "Agile Manifesto,"[1] in which the agile values and principles were described. Since then, many organizations have adopted and adapted the agile mindset to fit their needs in some or all their operations, including internal audit.

One of the key features in establishing the original agile mindset was creating a set of values and principles. The four values emphasized what was most crucial in the agile environment. As auditors, we have also adopted and adapted our version of the values and principles.

---

[1] Beck, K., et al. (2001) The Agile Manifesto. Agile Alliance. http://agilemanifesto.org/

DOI: 10.1201/9781003201571-1

Agile Audit Values

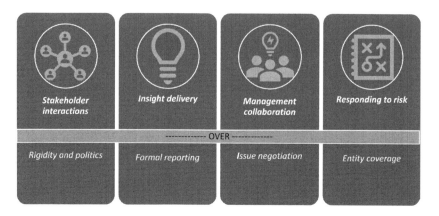

Figure 1.1   Agile Audit Values

Stakeholder Interactions Over Rigidity and Politics   In any organization, rigid adherence to a communication schedule and influence from internal politics restricts the flow of information from internal audit to management stakeholders who rely on the work done by audit. By placing more value on stakeholder interactions, we increase the flow of information to those who need it.

Insight Delivery Over Formal Reporting   Internal audit provides deep insights into the organization's risk exposure. All too often, the message is diluted or wholly lost as auditees argue with audit management over the verbiage in the audit report. When we focus on delivering insights, the substance of the message takes precedent over the format.

Management Collaboration Over Issue Negotiation   During most audits, control weaknesses will come to light. We should not waste time negotiating through the issue to serve the organization better by collaborating as a team with management. Internal audit has an advantage in that we know whom to involve in interdepartmental corrective actions.

Responding to Risk Over Entity Coverage   Providing insight into organizational risk is the goal of an internal audit. The audit universe, risk assessment, and resulting audit plan must be based on risk and not entities to reach this goal.

Agile Audit Principles

Similarly, agile principles were developed to add more detail to the values. Below are the 12 agile audit principles that we will follow. These principles maintain the spirit of the original principles, and each principle in this list is vitally important for the success of an agile audit department.

1. *Our highest priority is to support management's objectives by auditing critical and emerging risks.*
2. *Welcome changing requirements, even while executing the audit plan. Agile auditing accepts change for the best interest of the organization.*
3. *Deliver audit insights frequently, with real-time results during an audit and at least quarterly to the audit committee, with a preference for a shorter timescale.*
4. *Business managers and auditors must work together daily throughout the project.*
5. *Build audits around motivated individuals. Give them the environment and support they need, and trust them to get the job done.*
6. *The most efficient and effective method of conveying information to management and the audit team is face-to-face conversation.*
7. *Providing insight into the risk and control environment with senior leadership is the final measure of progress.*
8. *Agile auditing promotes a timely understanding of risk to operations. The first, second, and third lines of defense should maintain open communication and sharing of results.*
9. *Continuous attention to technical and soft skills enhances audit agility.*
10. *Simplicity—gaining insights into a risk and control environment without expanding the scope—is essential.*
11. *The best assessments, audits, and insights gained emerge from self-managing teams.*
12. *At regular intervals, the team reflects on becoming more effective, then trains and adjusts its processes accordingly.*

Agile Audit Transition

Historically, our audit plans were annual or multiyear listings of audit engagements. We measured our success by completing the plan on time and within budget. In a risk-based plan, we can quickly see that an annual plan is no longer acceptable. Our audit plans must be flexible and adapt to cover risks at a speed that makes sense for our organizations. The agile audit methodology creates an audit plan that meets the needs of a modern, risk-based team. Most of the guidance available on agile auditing emphasizes following the practice of agile development with internal audit as a stand-in for deliverable software. Often the practice involves having a scrum master, using scrum boards, burn-down charts, and managing epics. Introducing the new vocabulary and positions scares off more audit departments than it attracts. Using this guide, we will adopt an agile audit methodology without over-complicating the transition, taking a practical, audit-centric approach.

Agile auditing does not need to be overly complicated.

To begin, we need to define our objective for the transition to agile auditing. Once we have our objective in mind, we can move through the three primary phases of the audit lifecycle: planning, execution, and reporting/issue tracking. In each phase, we will make targeted changes to the traditional audit process to be agile in our approach. Some of the fundamental objectives include a change in mindset. As internal auditors, we shift our thinking from entity coverage to risk coverage and from delivering status updates to delivering organizational insights.

Table 1.1   Key points in the agile audit transition

TRADITIONAL INTERNAL AUDIT ⟹	AGILE AUDIT
Entity-based Audit Universe	Risk-based Audit Universe
Annual Risk Assessment and Planning	Quarterly Risk Assessment and Planning
Entity Coverage Focus	Emerging and Critical Risk Focus
Static Updates to Audit Committee	Continuous Insights for Audit Committee

As you will see throughout this book, many aspects of the transition depend on your department's size, goals, and level of maturity. No transition plan is universal, so we will present multiple options for you to consider, including discussion questions to facilitate internal conversations. This guide will also use a mix of internal audit and agile project management vocabulary to convey the most accurate meaning of the role or task. This book aims to improve the audit process, not turn you into a pure agile project manager. We will explain the agile terms and provide the audit correlation, and we will include terminology comparisons where applicable.

Agile Audit Benefits

Transitioning to agile audit has many profound benefits. The top five benefits that you should expect to gain from the move to agile audit include:

- Better alignment to management's expectations
- Deeper insights gained and shared during the audit process
- Increased interaction with auditees throughout the audit lifecycle
- Completing audits on time, on budget, and with higher quality results
- Improved communication within the audit team

Better Alignment

As we begin working with senior management during the audit plan development stage, the conversation starts with discussing risks that impact the organization's strategic goals and objectives. We are immediately elevating the conversation to the risks that matter most to management. We should then pivot to discussing emerging risks. We should have already performed research in this area so we can educate management when needed. Common areas to research emerging risks include literature from The IIA, external audit firms, industry journals, and competitors.

Deeper Insights

Since our focus is on understanding specific risks instead of end-to-end processes, we can dig deeper into specific areas and gain insight into the controls related to critical risks. These deeper insights are more valuable to the organization than the broad topics we previously covered.

Increased Interaction

Another aspect of the agile process is increased interaction with the auditee. We discussed including senior management in the planning process, but the interaction continues throughout the entire lifecycle. During fieldwork, we will hold daily standup meetings that include auditee participation. At the end of each audit section (sprint), we will include management in a review process that will take the form of an interim report review. At the end of the audit, we consolidate all interim results into a results review, and of course, we circle back and provide insight to the audit committee and the board.

Reduced Scope Creep

Because we are limiting our scope to specific risks and establishing a clear definition for audit completion, we control the extent of testing to the amount needed to gain insight. By doing so, we eliminate the possibility of scope creep. Also, during daily standup meetings, the team discusses all roadblocks, so the audit lead (scrum master) and the business contact can address and remove these roadblocks before this causes the team any delays.

Increased Communication

The auditors will also come together as a high-performing team. By setting aside time each day for the team to discuss progress and roadblocks, they each understand the work performed by the others. Sharing information increases the likelihood of eliminating overlap, increases the individual's understanding of the entire audit, and improves internal communication.

Agile Roles and Audit Equivalents

The agile audit method has unique roles and responsibilities. As mentioned before, we are not trying to force you into becoming an agile purist, so below, we have aligned typical agile roles and responsibilities to the most common audit roles. We will use the audit roles going forward.

Table 1.2 Agile Audit roles and Traditional Audit equivalents

AGILE ROLE	AUDIT ROLE	ROLE DETAILS
Product owner	Audit Plan Owner (CAE or Audit Director)	Owns ultimate responsibility for the audit plan.
Scrum master	Audit Lead (Audit Director or Manager)	Responsible for the audit project, assignments, daily standup meetings, results reviews, retrospectives, and informing the Audit Plan Owner.
Agile team	Audit Project Team	Executes the audit.
Stakeholders	Auditees/Senior Management	Audit's customer and recipient of the audit insights gained during the audit.
Technical and domain experts	SMEs within the audit team	Specialists within the audit team are more knowledgeable about a topic or technical skill (e.g., analytics).
Independent testing and audit team	Quality Assessment Team (Professional Practice)	Performs an internal evaluation or peer review of the work. Typically, only larger teams have this role.

Audit Plan Owner (Product Owner)

The Chief Audit Executive (CAE) or Audit Director owns primary responsibility for the audit plan. Developing the plan is done in conjunction with senior management. Since the groups are working closely together, the resulting audit plan addresses senior management's most urgent concerns. While not an exhaustive list, the Audit Plan Owner:

- Coordinates with senior management and the board to create and prioritize the audit plan
- Adjusts risks and audit priority continually to enable the delivery of highest value work
- Accepts or rejects work delivered by the team
- Determines insight reporting release cadence based on management's need and opportunity

Audit Lead (Scrum Master)

The Audit Lead performs a critical role in the audit process. During the audit, the Audit Lead organizes the team to address the risks in scope, conducts the daily standup meeting, facilitates the interim and the final review of results, and reports back to the Audit Plan

Owner. In an agile environment, the Audit Lead has several key responsibilities:

- Acts as a servant leader and the voice of the agile audit team
- Coaches team improvement in line with values, principles, and best practices
- Facilitates effective daily stand-up events, meetings, and retrospectives
- Enables close cooperation across all roles within the cross-functional team
- Assists Audit Plan Owner in preparing and refining the backlog
- Removes roadblocks
- Protects the team from external influence

Audit Project Team (Agile Team)

The Audit Project Team is the core of the entire process. The team is designed to explore the risks in scope, evaluate the controls, and determine if any issues need to be communicated back to management. Responsibilities include:

- Agile Audit Team is cross-functional with typically 3–5 people
- Defines, builds, tests, and delivers risk and control testing
- Members are dedicated to the specific value-stream delivery
- Some roles may be shared among multiple teams (e.g., Data Analytics, IT, Compliance)
- Plans for and commits to audit goals for each audit
- Applies quality review practices per IIA Standards
- Participates in agile events to deliver value, gather feedback, and ensure relentless improvement as an Agile Audit Team

SMEs (Technical and Domain Experts)

Subject Matter Experts (SMEs) are those individuals in the Audit Team who have unique skills and knowledge. While we often think of skills such as data analytics, these skills are not isolated to technical skills only. SMEs could be full members of the Agile Project Team or be brought in for specific testing.

Quality Assessment Team (Independent Testing Team)

Not all audit departments are large enough to sustain a full professional practice or quality assessment team, but all audit work must be reviewed.

Agile Terms and Audit Equivalents

Similarly, there are numerous terms used to describe many of the main features of an agile process. As in the prior table, the information below cross-references the agile and audit terminology.

Table 1.3   Agile Audit terms and Traditional Audit equivalents

AGILE TERM	AUDIT TERM	TERM DESCRIPTION (AGILE AUDIT)
Backlog	Draft Audit Plan	The list of audits we could perform. The backlog includes projects that may or may not end up in the final plan.
Epic	Final Audit Plan	A large grouping of audits is planned for a set duration of time.
Story	Audit	The audit department completes the work. The story's point is to convey the desired result; therefore, audits should focus on insights to share with senior management.
Timebox	Audit Schedule	Specific start and end dates for the audit and audit programs. The dates are firm.
Scope	Scope	What do the audit and team assignments cover? The audit's boundaries.
Burn-down Chart	None	A graphical representation of work left versus time.
Sprint	Audit Program	Subsections of an audit, ideally based on risks to review.
Sprint Review	Interim Issue Updates	Weekly/biweekly recap of scope, what went well, what needs improvement, and action plans.
Standup Meeting	None	Daily meeting to discuss progress and roadblocks that can include the audit team and auditees.

You will notice that several terms above have no audit equivalent. In this book, we will discuss the backlog when we discuss audit planning. Due to resource limitations, the backlog is listing audits we would like to do but cannot. A burn-down chart is a tool that larger agile audit departments sometimes use to show if blocked testing in an audit might cause completion to go beyond the scheduled end date.

Another is the standup meeting, a daily discussion of the progress and roadblocks encountered by each team member. We will cover all these terms in depth as we move through the audit lifecycle. For now, this is an introduction to the terms we will use.

Draft Audit Plan (Backlog)

After performing the risk assessment, we developed a list of audits we could perform. At this point, we are not committing to a plan as the backlog includes projects that may or may not end up in the final plan.

Final Audit Plan (Epic)

After prioritizing the draft audit plan, we settle on a final listing of audits we commit to perform within a defined period.

Audit (Story)

Each of the audits listed in the plan should include a well-defined, narrow scope that describes the risks the team will investigate. Audits are the agile equivalent of a story. The point of an agile story is to convey the desired result; therefore, audits should focus on insights to share with senior management.

Audit Schedule (Timebox)

The final audit plan, individual audits, and audit sprints operate within a fixed date range called a timebox. The dates are firm as the entire audit department will operate within synchronized cycles.

Scope

The scope of work is the audit's boundaries. By defining a narrow scope, we control the audit and team assignments amount of work. In agile auditing, the scope can be just one or two risks, unlike complete process audits in the traditional method.

Burn-Down Chart

While many audit progress reports exist, a burn-down chart is a unique graphical representation of the amount of work left versus the time left within the timebox.

Audit Program (Sprint)

Audit sprints are subsections of an audit. In some cases, the sprints may be made of audit programs or controls. Since we will focus on achieving a genuinely risk-based approach, the ideal sprint will be based on risks to review. Most often, sprints are one to two weeks long, with two-week sprints as the most common.

Interim Issue Updates (Sprint Review)

At the end of the sprint, the results must be shared with the auditee. These weekly/biweekly meetings recap the scope of work performed in the sprint, what went well, what needs improvement, and action plans. The audit team and the stakeholders attend to review the risks audited and issues found in the current sprint.

Daily Team Meeting (Daily Scrum)

The meeting includes the audit team and auditees. While a few audit managers already had the practice of daily team meetings, daily standup, or daily scrum is a special event. The meeting objective is to discuss progress and roadblocks, not to recap the past.

Discussion Questions

- Would you prefer to use audit-centric terminology or agile-centric terminology during your transition to agile audit? Consider the implications of both options.
- How do you think your auditees would react to being involved in a daily scrum meeting to discuss roadblocks to completing the audit?

- What audits have you participated in that included low-risk areas simply for the sake of process completeness? Did this lead to meaningful findings by the audit team?
- Thinking about the increased level of communication between the audit team members and the auditees, what additional benefits and challenges do you foresee for your organization?

Case Study

Each chapter of this book concludes with a case study. In the case study, we will follow the journey of a typical audit department that has embarked on the agile audit transformation journey. We will watch as they succeed in some areas and fail in others, and we will learn from their experiences. The case is derived from several real-world examples.

The Company

Aqua Junk, Inc.[2] is the world's premier manufacturer of recycled products made from ocean plastics, and junk washed up on the beach.

Aqua Junk, Inc

Figure 1.2 Aqua junk, Inc logo

Aqua Junk was founded in 2019 by a group of business professionals who wanted to leave the Earth cleaner for their children. They were sickened by reports of plastics in ocean garbage patches and the stomachs of sea creatures.

---

[2] This case study is a work of fiction. Names, characters, business, events, and incidents are the products of the author's imagination. Any resemblance to actual persons, living or dead, or actual events is purely coincidental, but we do hope there are companies with the same mission.

Aqua Junk makes various products, but their main product is a series of solid interlocking blocks used to create walls called Sea Walls. Sea Walls are purchased by state and city governments for municipal projects like highway noise reduction, companies who need to erect temporary office spaces, and homeowners for additional storage.

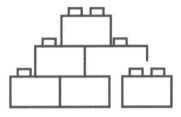

Figure 1.3 Aqua Junk product conceptualization

Aqua Junk's mission is to reverse the impact of ocean and river plastics on marine ecosystems by collecting and reusing the world's accumulated plastics. Five primary objectives support their mission:

1. Organize global efforts to capture and remove plastics from global waters
2. Reuse collected plastics for safe, long-term materials
3. Work with companies to eliminate the production of new, non-biodegradable consumer plastics
4. Incentivize industries to prevent equipment (e.g., commercial fishing nets) from abandonment
5. Coordinate efforts with like-minded organizations to gain global reach

The Internal Audit Team

The internal audit team has worked together for several years. They work well together and support the organization's overall mission. As a group, they participate in company-sponsored volunteering programs.

Gabi, the Chief Audit Executive, has nearly 20 years of experience in internal audit, external accounting, risk management, and systems controls. She has assembled a strong leadership team of directors and managers with diverse experience, education, and skills. The seniors on the team have three to five years' experience in internal audit, and some have advanced degrees and certifications. The staff auditors have been all newly hired in the past six months.

Here is the Internal Audit organization chart:

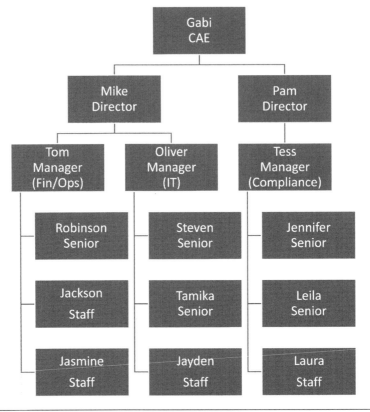

Figure 1.4 Aqua Junk's Internal Audit Organization Chart

At a recent IIA conference, Gabi attended a session on Agile Auditing, and she has read several interesting articles on the topic since. She then tasked Mike with organizing training for the department. A trainer was brought in to present to the team for two hours. After the training session, the team mostly agreed that moving to agile seemed like a great idea, but they were nervous. They were concerned that the auditees would take too long to get the supporting documentation. They were worried about missing something if they did not have a three-year plan to cover the entire organization.

Pam, the Compliance Director, was not convinced. She felt that compliance was not a good fit for agile auditing. Pam agreed to go along with the department in principle. Still, she made it very clear that her team would not jeopardize regulatory coverage for the sake of the agile initiative.

2
ASSESSING READINESS

Now that we have defined agile audit and gained an introduction to several concepts, the next step is to assess your department's readiness for the move to agile audit. Before we undertake to transform your internal audit department, we need to answer two questions: *can* you transition to agile audit, and *should* you transition to agile audit. In this chapter, we will start with an assessment to determine the department's readiness to move. From there, we will discuss the pros and cons of agile audit and how your organizational culture plays into the potential success or failure of that transition. Finally, we will review a list of common mistakes made in the transition so you can prepare for these scenarios.

> Agile auditing is not the answer for everyone, and there is no such thing as a "one size fits all" implementation of an agile mindset.

Assessing Your Department

Internal Audit

The assessment process starts with the internal audit department. It is often best to provide a baseline education to the team on agile auditing before beginning the assessment. Bring in a specialist to provide this training – this is not training based on a cursory understanding. Once the team understands the basics of agile auditing, take the pulse of the audit team to determine the level of fear, excitement, trepidation, and anxiety related to the topic. With the collective team's willingness to adopt agile auditing in mind, we must consider our stakeholders and the pros and cons of the transition.

DOI: 10.1201/9781003201571-2

Stakeholders

Next, we should take our other stakeholders into account. The stakeholders include the audit committee, our auditees, and the other assurance partners in the organization.

Audit Committee

The audit committee is our primary stakeholder. They must be consulted before embarking on the transition. The audit department is an extension of the audit committee. As they are concerned with overall governance and risk to the organization, the move to agile audit generally appeals to them as a worthwhile effort.

Auditees

The move to agile audit also impacts our auditees. They may be more involved in communication during the audit, and there is a good chance they will be subjected to audits with reduced notification. They will also be expected to produce documentation and to make time for interviews on a shorter timescale.

Assurance Partners

We also need to consider the broader assurance team. As you will learn in Chapter 9, a mature agile internal audit department relies on the work performed by other internal assurance providers for risk coverage. Sooner, rather than later, we need to ascertain our relationships to the other risk, control, and compliance teams. We also need to understand their appetite for working in an agile environment.

Finally, we consider the transition considering the potential outcomes: the pros and cons. Agile auditing is not the answer for everyone, and there is no such thing as a "one size fits all" implementation of an agile mindset. As you assess the department's readiness, it is easy to become swept up in the excitement of a new idea. Before we go too much further, it is time to slow down and consider why you may not want to move to agile auditing. To help, we have provided a pros and cons list to help you think about both sides of the argument.

Pros of Agile Auditing

Back in Chapter 1, we discussed the benefits of agile auditing. Just a reminder, we listed the top five benefits that you should expect to gain from the move to agile audit include:

- Better alignment to management's expectations
- Deeper insights gained and shared during the audit process
- Increased interaction with auditees throughout the audit lifecycle
- Completing audits on time, on budget, and with higher quality results
- Improved communication within the audit team

In addition to those benefits, there are several other items to add to the Pros list.

Flexibility

The most critical advantage of agile auditing is the flexibility it allows within the audit plan. The idea of setting an annual plan that requires board approval to change is not acceptable in a modern audit department. The entire premise behind agile auditing is to audit the risks that matter the most, and this prioritized list of risks will continually change. The audit committee and senior leadership will have a hard time arguing against this approach since it is in their best interest to use the audit department as a tactical team to explore the control environment in the areas of most significant concern.

Freedom to Stop

With flexibility comes the option to stop a project when the insights have been gained. Too often in the traditional process, we commit resources to test control operation effectiveness even after the design was determined to be flawed. By having a narrowly defined scope and the option to stop once the risk and controls are understood, we more efficiently and effectively use our limited time and resources.

Reduced Report Negotiation

An agile audit is performed in sprints of one or two weeks that end with reviewing the issues uncovered with management. Since this is done consistently throughout the audit, the final sprint review represents the audit closing meeting. At this point, there is very little arguing or negotiating over issues in the report as these have already been discussed.

Insights Provided to the Audit Committee

A significant advantage of agile auditing is the ability to produce real-time insight reports for the audit committee. Once all the audits are working on the same two-week cadence, all the sprint reviews occur simultaneously. This means the issues are ready for reporting and follow-up at the end of every two-week cycle. Assuming you have an issue tracking mechanism in place, the aggregated issues are ready for reporting in near real-time, with just a two-week lag. Of course, you are free to create a more formal reporting package for a quarterly meeting, but you have the option to provide more timely insights.

Cons of Agile Auditing

While agile auditing is a highly effective method for addressing risk-based auditing, there are valid reasons for remaining in a traditional audit methodology or possibly adopting a hybrid approach.

Hard Sell for Regulators

Perhaps the most common argument against agile auditing is the need to perform regulatory or statutory audits. For example, in banking, the regulators often require a three-year audit plan with evidence that the plan covers the entire organization. A quarterly plan is not going to support an agile plan that targets a quarterly planning cycle. For some, this means splitting the plan into regulatory audit and risk-based audits, and only the risk-based plan is agile.

Requires Retraining

The audit department will require training and coaching during the transition. Especially for long-term auditors, the shift to agile goes against years of experience in the traditional method. For some, the change may be too much. They can become frustrated and possibly leave the department.

Lack of Predictability

Many of us have experienced delays in getting documentation from control operators, and some of the documentation will inevitably be insufficient and lead to subsequent requests. There are also times when the one person you need to talk to is on vacation. In the end, audit timing is highly dependent on the team getting to the right people and the correct documentation, but people are unpredictable. Any delay can potentially derail the sprint cycle with a narrow scope audit in a short time frame.

Understanding Your Culture

Culture also plays an essential part in the success or failure of a transition to agile audit. For some organizations, the audit department is making this move as part of a larger initiative. In others, audit is blazing a new trail. In either case, the important point is to understand the environment in which you will be working.

Suppose you are working in the context of a larger initiative. In that case, the objective will be to align the values and principles, synchronize the audit sprints, and partner with the organization's scrum masters. On the other hand, if you are a trailblazer, you will need to educate the audit committee, and other stakeholders set clear expectations with the auditees, and find support from trained professionals.

Also, take the culture of the audit department itself into consideration. Your team may be open to change and ready to embrace agile auditing, or the team could be highly traditional, tenured auditors who are resistant to change. Acknowledging the cultural landscape allows you to plan more appropriately.

Avoiding Common Transition Pitfalls

Another tool in your readiness evaluation is planning for common pitfalls. Many other audit departments have already gone through this transition, and we can all learn from their lessons. Come back to this section if and *when* the inevitable mistakes happen.

Too Much Too Fast

When we layout the eventual transition plan, there will be multiple variations on the approach. In some cases, the approach takes on the full scope of all work completed by the audit department, from risk assessment to reporting, including every type of audit and consulting engagement. This approach is not going to work for everyone. If you take on more change than the team can absorb, the project will fail. For the transition to work, you should set a pace for change that works for your team.

Too Little Too Slow

Just like going too fast, you can also set a pace that is too slow and loses momentum. For example, you could transition fieldwork to an agile format to move planning and reporting later. If this goes on for more than a few months or even quarters, the team will become frustrated because the power of agile auditing comes from planning and scoping a much different type of audit.

Underestimating the Scrum Leader Role

The roles within the audit department will change with the agile audit implementation. Perhaps the most significant role change is the addition of the scrum master. The scrum master is commonly described as a servant leader whose job is to manage timelines, resolve problems, remove roadblocks, and coach the team members on agile audit methodologies. The scrum master is essential in an agile environment, making this one of the places that can fail in multiple ways if the role is underestimated.

Scrum masters need specialized training to perform their roles effectively. Especially in the transition from traditional to agile audit, we will turn auditors trained as project leads into a completely new role. Without proper training, we are setting them up to fail.

The other major cause for failure is overextending the scrum masters. There is a penchant for treating the scrum master like a lead auditor who reviews and prepares new audit work when reorganizing the department. Otherwise, the scrum master may be added to too many audits at once, reducing their effectiveness.

Team Rotation

Many audit departments operate on a team rotation basis. The benefit of this method is increased exposure to different management styles and the ability to create teams with specialized knowledge for each audit. The rotational structure works against you in an agile setting. With agile, the agile team dynamic requires the team to self-organize and work together like a well-oiled machine. Using rotational teams disrupts the necessary dynamic.

Lack of Training

Scrum masters are not the only ones who need training. The entire team is shifting to a new way of working. The department will need the training to develop an agile mindset and to undo many years of training and experience. Failure comes when audit leaders skip training due to scheduling and budgetary constraints. Training should include an overview of agile audit, role-based training, and audit phase training.

Inability to Scope Small Audits

When focused on specific risks, agile auditing yields a series of smaller scoped audits, at times an audit of a single risk. The ability to scope an audit of this nature requires a mindset shift. Early in the transition to agile audit, this can seem like too much change and scare away some more risk-averse auditors.

Fear of Missing Out

Another change that illicit fear is derived from the shift from an entity-based to a risk-based audit universe. Actual risk-based auditing is concerned with risk coverage, not entity coverage. There will likely be parts of the organization that are not included in the audit plan over a year. Once we understand that we are covering the most critical risks timely, the fear of missing entity coverage goes away.

Lack of Leadership Support

Support from the audit committee is required before we embark on the agile audit journey, but leadership support extends beyond this group. A successful transition to agile audit also requires support from operational management, who will be more closely involved with the audit team. Depending on your culture, this may require top-down direction, or the audit team may require bottom-up training and socializing.

Ceremony Over Substance

Some departments have already tried and failed to implement agile auditing. The most common reason given was a focus on ceremony over substance. When this happens, the focus was primarily on the fieldwork phase of the audit and almost entirely on the practice of holding scrum meetings, using a Kanban board, and conducting a retrospective. While these are essential elements of the process, the team failed to understand the purpose and objective of the event. Some teams understood the reasoning but drifted from the purpose or failed to follow through on action items from the retrospective. The lack of meaningful change leads to team frustration.

Settling Back Into Old Habits

The single most common cause for failure is falling back into our comfort zone. Typically, this slides back into the traditional method start in the daily scrum. When that meeting starts to become an update meeting, the scrum master's job is to bring this back to agile best practices. If this does not happen, the meeting loses any value, and this spiral can quickly take hold and undo the entire agile methodology.

Discussion Questions

- Consider the statement: "Agile auditing is not for everyone." How would you argue both for and against the transition to agile auditing for your organization?
- What is your department's stance on rotational audit teams?

- How do you feel about stopping an audit once the risks have been addressed versus continuing audit processes technically in scope with any remaining time?

Case Study

The internal auditors at Aqua Junk decided to charge forward with the idea of agile auditing after the initial training. One of the upcoming audits was selected since it was a well-known area that is audited every year.

Mike (Director) and Oliver (IT Audit Manager) chose an annual Critical System Access Audit as their agile audit pilot. From the two-hour training they had attended, they knew the following:

- Agile projects are organized into sprints
- Agile teams have a scrum master that keeps the project moving
  - The scrum master holds a daily sprint meeting with the team
  - The scrum master holds a retrospective at the end of the project
- Project tasks are laid out on a scrum board or Kanban board

With that information, Oliver and his team set off to perform the audit. On Monday, Oliver pulled up the standard audit program the team had used for the past few years, wrote out each test procedure onto a sticky note, and put all the tests into a TO DO column on a whiteboard in the office.

He assigned himself the role of scrum master and instructed his team to choose their first test procedure. As these are complete, move the sticky note to the DONE column. He would review the test and then move the note to the REVIEWED column. In this way, they should get through the audit faster than the prior year.

On Tuesday, the team started with a daily scrum meeting. Oliver asked, "What did you get done yesterday?"

Steven pointed to the whiteboard, which showed that none of the tests had been completed.

The same thing happened on Wednesday and then again on Thursday.

On Friday, the fifth day of the audit, Oliver was supposed to hold a sprint review, but nothing was done yet. Frustrated, he asked the team what the problem was. He then found out that the application administrators they were auditing were out of the office at a team training event, and they would not be back until the following week.

Oliver decided to go back to the traditional way of auditing. He assigned the prewritten audit program in sections as it had been created and set the team back to work. The audit took two weeks longer than usual.

The team was asked to report back to Gabi on the pilot. When Oliver explained how the entire agile process was broken, in his opinion, Gabi listened intently.

She asked him what risks were the highest priority in the audit – he could not answer.

She asked him if he had asked roadblocks the team was facing on the first day – he said he had not.

She asked him if the auditee had been invited to the daily scrum meeting – he said they were not.

Gabi realized that several mistakes had been made before the audit ever started. The team was not prepared, and they were not even close to adequately trained. Instead of criticizing the pilot team, Gabi made plans to correct the mistakes. Over the next few weeks, she spoke with agile audit specialists who would help her redesign the audit department and reshape the team's mindset to one of agility.

Gabi chose Avery, an agile audit consultant who seemed to understand what she wanted to accomplish and what the team had tried to do independently. The plan she and the consultant created would touch every aspect of the audit lifecycle over 12 weeks. The plan also included coaching, extensive training for scrum masters, basic agile audit training for the entire team, and support explaining the new way of working to the other stakeholders.

3
AGILE AUDIT LIFECYCLE

Now we move into the audit process. Chapter 3 compares/contrasts the traditional process to the agile process. The bulk of the chapter then gives a high-level description of agile audit processes through the entire audit lifecycle. The following five chapters are a deep dive into each step of the lifecycle.

Traditional vs. Agile Audit Lifecycle

The traditional audit lifecycle, as illustrated below, is linear. The process starts with a risk assessment to determine a plan, and it ends with reporting to the audit committee about the status of that plan and identified issues. For many audit departments, management focuses heavily on audit plan completion.

Traditional Audit Lifecycle

In the traditional model, the audit department uses information from the risk assessment, primarily based on interviews with management and ratings provided by the audit management, to build the annual audit plan. They also include any required audits and potentially any management requests. The audit department presents the plan to the audit committee for approval, and from there, the plan is set for the year. Audits are next spread across the year, considering risks included in the audit, logistics, and impact to the auditee. The audit report is issued at the end of the audit, and findings move into a follow-up phase. At the end of each quarter, the audit department creates a status update for the audit committee.

DOI: 10.1201/9781003201571-3   **25**

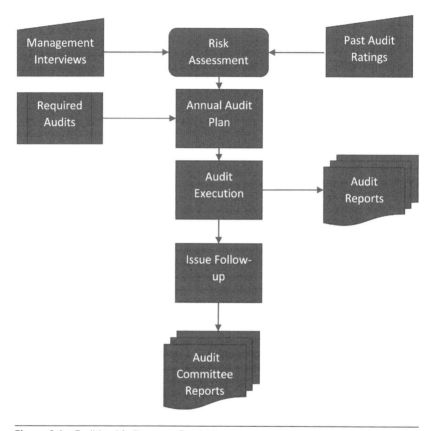

Figure 3.1 Traditional Audit process flowchart

Agile Audit Lifecycle

The agile audit lifecycle, as shown above, is circular in nature. The distinguishing feature of the agile process is an information feedback loop that updates the risk assessment with new information learned during the audit, deliberate inclusion of emerging risks, risk ranking required audits, and quarterly planning.

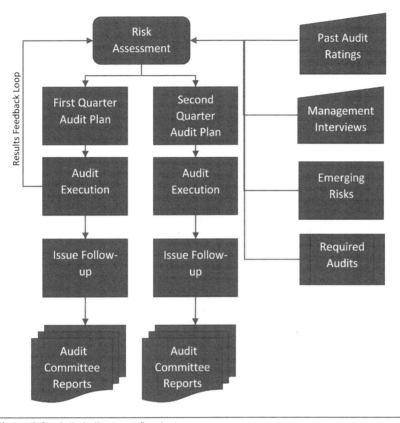

Figure 3.2 Agile Audit process flowchart

You may have noticed that the audit report is missing from the diagram above. The IIA Standards do not require the audit report. Audit reports are unnecessary for the agile audit process and can be replaced with a simple review session. As always, you know your culture best and can decide to keep the audit report. We will get deeper into this discussion later and will discuss both options.

Agile Audit Risk Assessment

The agile audit risk assessment evaluates a risk-based audit universe to determine the relative risk ranking of the risks that matter most to the management at a point in time. The assessment should support the first agile audit principle to *support management's objectives by auditing critical and emerging risks*. The risk assessment must be revisited frequently, at least quarterly, with a goal for continuous risk assessment as the process matures to meet the first principle.

> Agile Audit Principle 1: Our highest priority is to support management's objectives by auditing critical and emerging risks.

Agile Audit Plan

The prioritized risks derived from the assessment are organized into possible audits. This backlog of possible audits represents the agile audit plan. The backlog should be ranked based on the risk levels that came from the assessment.

Agile Audit Capacity Planning and Scheduling

Once the backlog of audits is developed, the team schedule for the next quarter can be created based on capacity. The projects should ideally all operate on a synchronized sprint cadence. Having a synchronized cadence will facilitate coordination across the teams and with the production of audit committee insights.

Agile Audit Execution

During fieldwork, the teams execute the audits by working through the prioritized risks in scope for their projects. The work is led by a scrum master who manages the workload, monitors the timeline, removes obstacles, and coaches the team. The scrum master will conduct daily stand-up meetings and report to the CAE during a scrum of scrums meeting. Scrum masters also facilitate a sprint review to discuss issues raised during the audit and gather management action plans. At the end of the audit, the scrum master will conduct a retrospective with the audit team to find areas for continuous improvement.

Agile Audit Reporting

Audit reporting is broken into two phases: the audit report and management insight reporting. During the audit, issues are uncovered and discussed with management. The issues are brought to the management's attention in near real-time, ideally during a daily scrum meeting and again in the sprint review. The goal during the audit is to gather the action plan and set the mitigation process into motion during the audit. Getting to this point turns creating the audit report into a recap exercise that needs very little discussion, making the formal report an unnecessary, redundant effort.

Audit Committee insight reporting is the goal and main objective for the audit department. By capturing the issues and discussing with management during each sprint, the audit department can collect, categorize, consolidate, and report on issues and issue trending by the related risks at the end of each sprint cycle. The regular cadence means that a department on a two-week sprint cycle can provide insight to the audit committee on the most critical risks to the organization every two weeks. In internal audit, achieving the goal of delivering continuous insights is likely the most valuable contribution we can make to any organization.

Discussion Questions

- Since the agile audit lifecycle still includes all the elements of the traditional lifecycle, does this set you at ease when thinking about the transformation?
- How do you address emerging risks into your current risk assessment?
- What other sources do you capture for your audit plan risk assessment?
- How long does it take to complete your current risk assessment? Why does it take that long?
- How much time goes into presentations and reporting to the audit committee?

- Thinking about your current audit lifecycle, how long does it take to complete an audit from start to finish? For the discussion, consider the start of the audit from when the engagement/ announcement letter is sent out and call the audit completed when the final audit report is published.

Case Study

Avery, the agile audit consultant, provided general training to the entire team on the differences between traditional and agile auditing. During the training session, Mike spoke up about his concerns. Mike was worried about the risk assessment process. As he explained, the current risk assessment takes about two months. Six weeks are spent on the assessment and interviews. The team then spends at least a week creating the plan, another week making the audit committee presentation, and then the audit committee sometimes changes the plan in the first quarter meeting. How could this possibly work with quarterly risk assessments?

Pam also spoke up about her concerns with compliance audits. She again said that the audits are mandatory, so she did not know how compliance would fit into the agile way of working.

Tom jumped in as well. He voiced his worries about fieldwork and reporting. How could fieldwork stay on track if the documentation did not arrive on time? With reporting, everyone knows audit reports take at least a month after the audit to finalize. At this point, the rest of the department also spoke up. While everyone thought the idea of agile auditing made sense, no one could see how it could work in the real world.

Avery wrote all the team's concerns on the whiteboard in the training room. He assured them that these concerns are common in the transition to agile audit and that subsequent training and practice exercises would cover all these topics and much more.

4

AGILE AUDIT RISK
ASSESSMENT

For many audit departments, the first step on the transition journey is audit planning. Audit planning is one of the most complex areas to transition, but it is arguably the most important. Adding to the complexity is the fact that every department has a different approach to traditional planning.

Agile audit planning facilitates an audit plan that addresses the most urgent risks that impact our organization. Given that the world is unpredictable and risks can emerge in new forms with unknown results, our planning needs to encompass a smaller time window. We should start by reducing our annual plan down to a quarterly plan. We will include mandatory audits that we must complete in that quarter and the highest rated risks to audit for the next quarter.

> The ability to shift plans quickly and audit based on emerging risks that threaten the organization from achieving its objectives is the cornerstone of agile auditing.

In the most typical traditional audit process, the audit department begins by assessing what they believe represents everything they could audit within the organization. The resulting audit universe is often comprised of processes or departments. The auditors will then start a process of risk ranking the potential areas to audit. The ranking process varies since there is very little guidance on the subject.

Rethinking the Audit Universe

The audit universe will change to include the organization's most critical objectives and risks in an agile audit environment. Since new risks constantly emerge and organizations modify objectives to meet global

DOI: 10.1201/9781003201571-4

changes, the audit department must also react quickly. The ability to shift plans quickly and audit based on emerging risks that threaten the organization from achieving its objectives is the cornerstone of agile auditing. In agile terms, the audit plan is an epic that splits into smaller stories (audits).

To illustrate the point, we can see how our case study company modifies its audit universe and performs a risk assessment. Starting with the audit universe, we will move from an entity-based organizational structure to one that includes the strategic objectives and risks. Like most companies, Aqua Junk's traditional audit universe utilizes the organization's functional structure. Internal audit adopted the same format since the organization already uses the structure.

In an agile audit, we do not need to focus on the functional structure. Our goal is not to "audit accounting"; we aim to provide management insights into the risks impacting strategic objectives. When Aqua Junk decided to rethink the audit universe, they started with the five primary objectives that management developed to support the mission statement, and then they gathered the known risks. Here is the original and resulting audit universe:

Table 4.1   Traditional audit universe compared to an Agile Audit risk universe

TRADITIONAL AUDIT UNIVERSE	RISK-BASED AUDIT UNIVERSE
Aqua Junk, Inc	Aqua Junk, Inc
Finance	Organize global efforts to capture and remove plastics from global waters
Planning	
Budgeting	Finding people willing and able to collect the materials
Treasury	Purchasing equipment capable of collecting the materials
Reporting	Protecting employees enduring harsh working conditions
Risk Management	Protecting equipment from harsh environmental conditions
Accounting	Reuse collected plastics for safe, long-term materials
Accounts Payable	Develop cost-effective production methods
Accounts Receivable	Meet environmental safety concerns with products
Tax	Ability to sell the product while covering costs
Human Resources	Maintaining eco-friendly shipping methods for finished products
Recruiting	Work with companies to eliminate the production of plastics
Compensation	Resistance from government entities
Training	Resistance from industrial interests
Health and Safety	Lack of brand awareness and market presence
Marketing	Incentivize industries to prevent equipment abandonment
Content Marketing	Unwillingness to partner with the company
Customer Service	Unable to meet our sustainability standards
Advertising	Damage to reputation through partner relationships

(Continued)

Table 4.1   Traditional audit universe compared to an Agile Audit risk universe *(Continued)*

TRADITIONAL AUDIT UNIVERSE	RISK-BASED AUDIT UNIVERSE
Technology	Coordinate efforts with like-minded organizations to gain global reach
Application Development	
IT Management	Unwillingness to form partnerships
IT Security	
User Support and Service	

Starting with Strategic Risks

As you can see, the new audit universe is based on risks to the organization. The auditors will add additional risks to this structure, but they will always add these risks in the context of strategic objectives. When they are building out the risk-based universe, they will pull information from many sources. One of the best places to start is with the strategic risks listed in the financial statements. Aqua Junk, like all public companies, lists risks in the financial statements. In the most recent 10-K, in "Item 1A. Risk Factors", the following risk is included: *"The failure to attract and retain additional qualified personnel or to maintain our eco-centric company culture could harm our business and culture and prevent us from executing our business strategy."*

In a traditional audit environment, we would rarely concern ourselves with the idea of sourcing talent. We would typically stick to financial and basic operational concerns. Under an agile methodology, we would include this talent risk (based on Aqua Junk's 10-K) on the audit plan since it is a significant organizational concern. The risk impacts the first strategic objective since we need the right people to achieve the objective. For the internal auditors, the audit could include questioning management's level of insight into the talent competition landscape, efforts in innovation, new market entrants who are also hiring, employee diversity, wage comparisons for the location and industry, and other factors related to hiring talented employees.

Incorporating Emerging Risks

Our risk assessment should be a continuous effort, and we should formalize updates at least every quarter. If we only consider risks to the organization annually, we will not adequately serve our stakeholders.

In Aqua Junk's case, we could perform a risk assessment in December of one year with a plan to audit the risk in September. A direct competitor could enter the market in January and hire the top 200 local candidates. The level of talent sourcing risk would have increased, but our assessment was out of date before we ever began the audit.

In addition to the apparent objectives and risks often present in the annual financial statements, we should also have emerging risks always on our agenda. Emerging risks are those risks the organization was likely not prepared to control. Auditors should be aware of events going on in the world that could impact our organizations. For example, the pandemic risk was probably not on anyone's risk assessment or audit plan in 2019. The events in the first quarter of 2020 led nearly every audit department to add this emerging risk and soon after a Business Continuity Plan audit to their audit plan.

Emerging risks are challenging – it is both difficult to identify and to understand the risks. Keeping up with risk trends helps to follow emerging risk thought leadership from sources like the IIA and global consulting firms. Other good sources include news sites that allow you set up alerts and your competitor's financial statements.

The act of performing an audit also puts you as close to the front lines as possible. In the audit, you will uncover new risks, controls that are poorly designed or not operating correctly, as well as a host of other issues. We must incorporate information and insights gained into the risk assessment for future consideration.

In the agile plan, we project out just one-quarter at a time. By bringing in risks related to strategic objectives, emerging risks, and updated understanding from completed audits, we build a more comprehensive risk view of the organization quarter over quarter for the agile plan.

Since we cannot afford to audit low-risk areas, we can use exploratory testing and analytics to develop the plan. For example, we have an emerging reputational risk related to the disparity in pay among genders. Instead of launching a full audit, we could perform exploratory analytics to analyze this one risk. In this approach, we could pull the data, perform the data analytics, and decide if the results warrant adding an audit to the plan for that quarter. If the answer is no, we could choose to create a memo with the test results to management. If we add the audit to the plan, we have a head start on the test work.

Management Interviews

To help management think through strategic and emerging risks, consider the types of questions and conversations you will have with management. They need to think beyond the company itself and consider risks they have never dealt with before. One way to facilitate the thought process around emerging risks is to break the world into categories, such as people, equipment, and technology.

The questions might look like the list below:

- People
  - How has the current political climate impacted your organization?
  - What new competitors are entering your market?
  - Has there been management or key employee turnover?
  - Has management implemented any process changes?
  - Were there any recent events that impacted employee morale?
  - Are there any impending changes that will impact the staff?
  - Are employees balancing work and home responsibilities well?
  - Does the organization provide appropriate learning opportunities?
  - Are managers trained to provide feedback?
- Equipment
  - Is new equipment introduced that may require a learning curve?
  - Are there any tools in use approaching the end of their useful life?
  - How many service calls has the staff made recently to address faulty equipment?
  - Does the team have the equipment they need to accomplish their work?
  - Is the end-of-life policy reasonable?
  - Do individuals supplement with personal equipment when they do not have what they need?
- Technology
  - Which new technology and cybersecurity threats need addressing?
  - Have new system implementations recently started or finished?
  - Are people finding system workarounds for the technology they do not like or do not understand?

- Do departments have the authority to acquire needed technology?
- Is there a clear organizational technology strategy?

Risk Self-Assessments

A tool that may help you consider changes to the risk assessment is risk self-assessments with management. There are several variations regarding risk self-assessment techniques, but in general, there are three standard methods for performing the evaluations:

- Facilitated workshops
- Surveys or questionnaires
- Management analysis

A facilitated workshop is a dynamic, participative event led by a facilitator in which the organization's management is actively engaged in a discussion about risks and controls. The objective of the facilitated workshop is to engage management in a discussion that leads to an evaluation of the effectiveness of the controls the organization has in place and ultimately to gain consensus on whether all related business objectives will be met with the controls that were examined.

Surveys are more straightforward methods that can be used to good effect without too much effort. The surveys should be designed much like the risk assessment to help consolidate the gathered information. Anonymous surveys are helpful in areas where you are trying to gather comments as well. People may be more likely to discuss concerns.

Management Analysis is often used as self-testing or peer testing. Control owners will sometimes test the control on their own to validate the control is working as intended to validate the effectiveness and correct any issues proactively.

Performing the Assessment

Typically, during the risk assessment, the audit universe is risk-rated in one of three ways: at the entity level, as a category of risk, or at the process level. All three are flawed.

1. The entity is rated with a simple high, moderate, or low rating.

Table 4.2   Entity level risk assessment

EXAMPLE	DEPARTMENT	RISK RATING
Entity Risk Level	Human Resources	High

The entity risk level is much too high to perform a meaningful audit. A risk assessment of this type would lead to an end-to-end audit of the entity.

2. The entity has high-level risk categories associated and rated.

Table 4.3   Category level risk assessment

EXAMPLE	DEPARTMENT	RISK	RISK RATING
Categorical Risk Level	Human Resources	Strategic risk	High
		Operational risk	Moderate
		Financial risk	Moderate

A categorical risk assessment is too vague for auditors to focus their work. Using the example above, the audit would start with all strategic risks that could impact Human Resources. This audit would include deep-dive inspections of all aspects of the employee cycle: hiring, training, learning and development, assessments, promotions, pay, terminations, and probably much more.

3. The entity has detailed, process-level risks associated and rated.

Table 4.4   Process level risk assessment

EXAMPLE	DEPARTMENT	RISK	RISK RATING
Process Risk Level	Human Resources	Hiring practices	Low
		Appropriate pay	High
		Employee retention	Moderate

The process risk level is better since the risk statements are more defined. In this example, an audit of pay appropriateness could still lead to a broad scope that includes discrimination, market comparisons, evaluations, and more.

Occasionally, auditors will then factor in financial statement accounts to add financial materiality into the assessment. In the end, we select the highest-rated entities as targets for the annual audit plan.

While many auditors call the approach "risk-based planning," they perform entity-based audit planning in practice. In all three examples above, the assessment's base, or starting point, was an entity-oriented audit universe, not risks.

The first time we make this shift, we should start with the most critical risks to management achieving their strategic objectives. Based on our risk assessment, with input from financial statements, conversations with senior management, and completed audits, we should plan to audit the highest-rated strategic and emerging risks. Next, we must consider noncompliance with regulatory requirements as a significant risk and include any required regulatory audits. The list of risks represents the potential audit plan for that quarter. We would then trace those risks to the underlying processes to determine the scope of the audit.

Within a company's 10-K, we can look to the section titled "*Item 1A – Risk Factors*" for information about the most concerning management risks. We can also see examples in annual reports, websites, business plans, objective statements, and strategy guides.

To facilitate the conversation, we will continue with our case study. Aqua Junk's website states a clear mission:

"Aqua Junk's mission is to reverse the impact of ocean and river plastics on marine ecosystems through the collection and reuse of the world's accumulated plastics."

For the audit department to truly add value to the company, they should be auditing toward this objective.

In Aqua Junk's financial statement, the company details its most concerning risks. The very first of which reads:

"We are expanding our ocean plastic retrieval operations in remote areas of the world where local resistance may be met and harsh environmental conditions encountered, requiring increased precautions for protecting employee safety."

If we are designing an audit approach that aligns with Aqua Junk's strategic objective, the plan would include controls related to this risk. The audit should include a review of safety controls, including the operations safety plan to address this risk.

Below is an example of how the audit could start to take shape:

Table 4.5   Example audit with strategic objectives

AUDIT	STRATEGIC OBJECTIVE	STRATEGIC RISK
Employee Safety Audit	Organize global efforts to capture and remove plastics from global waters	Employee safety while removing plastics in remote areas of the world where local resistance may be met and harsh environmental conditions encountered

During the audit, we would then dive deeper into the specific detail-level risks that would come out during a walkthrough. The initial interview could start with questions such as:

- What steps were taken to ensure the maximum level of plastics is safely removed from the water on each trip? [Relates to the Strategic Objectives and Risks]
- What would disrupt the retrieval process? How likely is this to happen, and how bad would it be if it did happen? What are the most dangerous elements of the trip from an employee safety point of view? [Dives deeper into the Detailed Risks and follows with management's assessment rating for impact and likelihood]
- What have you done to prevent the events that can injure employees from happening? [Articulates the Controls in place for the Detailed Risks]

Now the risks need prioritization. In a traditional risk assessment, we may include several qualitative and quantitative risk metrics to exclude the low-ranked risks from consideration. The task is a little different in agile auditing. Since the audit has a smaller scope, some audits can be completed relatively quickly, making room for the subsequent risk to audit. The goal of the risk assessment is not to create High-, Moderate-, and Low-risk buckets; the goal in the agile assessment is to rank all the risks relative to each other in a list from the highest to the lowest. Since this is the goal, we can use simpler scoring metrics like Impact and Likelihood, or you can continue to use more complex measures. A word of caution, however, the more complexity you add, the longer the assessment will take, and you will only have one to two weeks to complete the assessment. Remember, the assessment is just a tool to aid in prioritization, not the end product. Below is an example of the risk assessment scored using impact and likelihood.

Table 4.6 Risk-based audit universe

RISK-BASED AUDIT UNIVERSE	IMPACT	LIKELIHOOD	SCORE
Organize global efforts to capture and remove plastics from global waters			8.75
Finding people willing and able to collect the materials	5	2	10
Purchasing equipment capable of collecting the materials	5	2	10
Protecting employees enduring harsh working conditions	5	3	15

(Continued)

Table 4.6   Risk-based audit universe   *(Continued)*

RISK-BASED AUDIT UNIVERSE	IMPACT	LIKELIHOOD	SCORE
Protecting equipment from harsh environmental conditions	5	1	5
Reuse collected plastics for safe, long-term materials			7
Develop cost-effective production methods	4	1	4
Meet environmental safety concerns with products	5	2	10
Ability to sell the product while covering costs	2	4	8
Maintaining eco-friendly shipping methods for finished products	1	1	1
Work with companies to eliminate the production of new plastics			4.33
Resistance from government entities	3	3	9
Resistance from industrial interests	2	1	2
Lack of brand awareness and market presence	1	2	2
Incentivize industries to prevent equipment from abandonment			2.33
Unwillingness to partner with the company	3	1	3
Unable to meet our sustainability standards	2	1	2
Damage to reputation through partner relationships	2	1	2
Coordinate efforts with like-minded organizations to gain global reach			2
Unwillingness to form partnerships	2	1	2

The assessment used a 5-point scale for each risk (1=low, 5=high), a total risk score (impact x likelihood), and an aggregated average for each strategic objective.

For audit planning purposes, we can extract the risks and rank these priority orders. The list of prioritized risks is essentially the audit plan.

Table 4.7   Prioritized risk ranking

RISK PRIORITIZATION	IMPACT	LIKELIHOOD	SCORE
Protecting employees enduring harsh working conditions	5	3	15
Finding people willing and able to collect the materials	5	2	10
Purchasing equipment capable of collecting the materials	5	2	10
Meet environmental safety concerns with products	5	2	10
Resistance from government entities	3	3	9
Ability to sell the product while covering costs	2	4	8
Protecting equipment from harsh environmental conditions	5	1	5
Develop cost-effective production methods	4	1	4
Unwillingness to partner with the company	3	1	3
Resistance from industrial interests	2	1	2
Lack of brand awareness and market presence	1	2	2
Unable to meet our sustainability standards	2	1	2
Damage to reputation through partner relationships	2	1	2
Unwillingness to form partnerships	2	1	2
Maintaining eco-friendly shipping methods for finished products	1	1	1

For those who go further, the next logical step may be to create a Risk/Control Matrix (RCM) that includes more detailed risks and any known controls:

Table 4.8   Example risk and control matrix

STRATEGIC OBJECTIVE	STRATEGIC RISK	DETAILED RISK	CONTROL(S)
Organize global efforts to capture and remove plastics from global waters	Protecting employees enduring harsh working conditions	Outdated marine equipment could strand employees in the middle of the ocean	Perform deep maintenance checks before retrieval trips Qualified technicians are onboard every vessel No equipment is maintained past its useful life

The identified controls will eventually lead to test procedures during audit execution to validate the design and operating effectiveness of the controls, like the example below. As we complete testing and document any issues we find, we can now provide reporting to management and the audit committee that shows issues tied to strategic risks and company objectives.

Table 4.9   Example controls with test procedures

CONTROL	TEST PROCEDURE
Perform deep maintenance checks before retrieval trips	Review preventative maintenance logs compared to all repair logs.
Qualified technicians are onboard every vessel	Review ship logs for personnel. Verify technician's credentials.
No equipment is maintained past its useful life	Verify that all equipment in use is within the documented helpful life period. Validate the useful life records are accurate.

When we take the approach detailed above, we directly connect the work we do in audit execution to the strategic plan. This approach is crucial if we are going to achieve the critical improvement of alignment to strategy. By providing this extremely important information, we are all elevating the nature of the audit work, positioning our departments as true trusted advisors to management.

Discussion Questions

- What type of assessment is your department currently producing?
- When was the last time your audit universe was overhauled entirely?

- How can you incorporate emerging risks into the risk assessment?
- What are some sources where you can find ideas for emerging risks that can impact your organization?

Case Study

Gabi knew she needed to discuss a major change in the audit approach with the audit committee. Before taking the agile transition much further, she decided to call the audit committee chair. Gabi explained the basic concept of what the shift to agile audit would include. The audit committee chair commented that the change made sense to him, but the full committee should better understand what this would mean to the organization. Since the next audit committee meeting was several months away, he offered to set up a virtual meeting to discuss this one topic.

Gabi's presentation included a basic overview of business agility and agile auditing and the proposed changes to the audit universe and risk assessment. At first, several committee members expressed concern over audit coverage if the audit universe no longer focuses on the standard corporate structure. Gabi explained that the new model would still provide coverage from a risk perspective instead of a departmental one. The approach would provide better risk assurance for the organization since less time would be spent on low-risk areas. Another benefit, she explained, is that the risks would not be limited to a specific entity, allowing the team to audit across functions to understand the control environment better. She then presented the new risk universe:

Table 4.10 Example risk-based universe

RISK-BASED AUDIT UNIVERSE

Aqua Junk, Inc
  Organize global efforts to capture and remove plastics from global waters
    Finding people willing and able to collect the materials
    Purchasing equipment capable of collecting the materials
    Protecting employees enduring harsh working conditions
    Protecting equipment from harsh environmental conditions
  Reuse collected plastics for safe, long-term materials
    Develop cost-effective production methods
    Meet environmental safety concerns with products

(Continued)

Table 4.10   Example risk-based universe *(Continued)*

RISK-BASED AUDIT UNIVERSE
Ability to sell the product while covering costs
Maintaining eco-friendly shipping methods for finished products
Work with companies to eliminate the production of plastics
Resistance from government entities
Resistance from industrial interests
Lack of brand awareness and market presence
Incentivize industries to prevent equipment abandonment
Unwillingness to partner with the company
Unable to meet our sustainability standards
Damage to reputation through partner relationships
Coordinate efforts with like-minded organizations to gain global reach
Unwillingness to form partnerships

At this point, the group discussed the advantages of aligning the audit plan directly to corporate strategy and objectives. The audit committee agreed this was a good approach and decided to move forward with the option to revisit the conversation later in the year after internal audit has had a chance to pilot the program.

5

AGILE AUDIT PLANNING

Up to this point in the agile audit methodology, the focus has been on creating a risk assessment that identifies the organization's most critical, time-sensitive risks. Now that we have the listing, we need to create an agile approach to scheduling the audit work for the team.

Backlog Development

The starting point for this phase of the audit lifecycle is the prioritized listing of risks we produced during the risk assessment. The listing is now our backlog of risks to audit. The department leaders should review the backlog of risks for natural groupings. The groupings of risks will constitute the audit. By the end of the review, there may be audits with just one risk, and other audits may have multiple risks. The way you choose to group risks into audits will vary depending on your organization and the nature of the risks. For many, the grouping of risks may come down to the risk and control owners. We still must work within the organization. We do not want to add to audit fatigue by coming back repeatedly to the same individuals if we could have reviewed several risks under their management at once.

User Story Development

A standard tool in agile project management is the user story. When agile was first used in software development, user stories were created to tell the story of the business user of the software wanted from a new feature. In agile audit, we may find it helpful to develop user stories to describe the audit's planning considerations (IIA Standard 2201), objective (IIA Standard 2210), and scope (IIA Standard 2220). The story for each audit will help you estimate the time commitment and resource allocation. Agile stories have three elements: who, what, and why. We can phrase the audit story as, "Management would like to understand the organization's risk exposure related to ___ because ___."

Next, we estimate the mix of resources needed for the audit. Audit resources will include two elements: hours and skills. The agile audit team is comprised of people who have specific skills and limited availability. Audits are assigned to the teams with the best fit of both availability and skills.

Audit Prioritization

Audit prioritization should follow the same concepts as risk prioritization. If risks were grouped to create the audit, maintain the priority of the highest-rated risks for the audit risk level. The relative ranking can be kept at a categorical level (high, moderate, low), or you may find it easier to assign a numeric score for more clarity.

Capacity Planning

During capacity planning, you are estimating how many audits an agile team can realistically achieve. The department may be split into several teams, so it is easier to develop individual team backlogs.

The resulting plan from the risk assessment will initially include two main audit types: mandatory and risk-based. The list of audits will probably be much longer than you can handle, so we need to decide which audits to complete in the current quarter, which audits to postpone, and which we can drop. Below is an example of a list of potential audits. For our discussion, let's assume these are all rated as high risk:

Table 5.1 List of example audits

MANDATORY AUDITS	RISK-BASED AUDITS
SOX Audit	Employee Safety at Work
GDPR Audit	Talent Acquisition
	Equipment Acquisition
	Product Environmental Safety
	Resistance From Government Entities
	Product Pricing and Marketing
	Equipment Protection

We have ten potential audits on the list, and in a perfect world, we would perform them all. Unfortunately, we have limited resources. We can run an estimation simulation for the audit plan to determine our capacity using a theoretical department with 15 auditors.

Remember, we are only projecting out one quarter. The simulation below starts with several common assumptions:

1. The total hours per person is 2080 (40 hours/week * 52 weeks)
2. Since we are evaluating one quarter, the base hours are 520 (2080/4)
3. Each staff level has different audit work allocations with time set aside for administrative tasks
4. We will include one manager per team with a mix of seniors and staff

Table 5.2 Example calculation for total audit hours

RESOURCES	COUNT	AVAILABLE HOURS	CALCULATION
Chief Audit Executive	1	NA	CAE not directly involved in audits
Audit Directors	2	260	25% allocation for audit review (((2080/4)*2)*.25))
Audit Managers	3	1170	75% allocation to perform audit and review (((2080/4)*3)*.75)
Senior Auditors	5	2080	80% allocation to perform audit (((2080/4)*5)*.80)
Staff Auditors	4	1872	90% allocation to perform audit (((2080/4)*4)*.90)
Total hours for quarter		**5382**	

Scheduling Timeboxing

For our quarter, we want to have each team perform two audits, which will amount to two audits lasting five weeks with a week at the end of each for administrative tasks for each team. In agile terms, five weeks is our timebox. Timeboxing means that at the end of the five weeks, we end the audit.

The resulting audit plan may look like the illustration below. The plan excludes Audit Directors as each audit will get approximately 32 hours of review from a director. At the beginning of the planning process, we had ten potential audits, but our capacity only allows the completion of six audits. If the audits we start with can be completed sooner, we may pull these audits in quicker. If the audit is completed on time and the team cannot execute the four audits, these will move to the backlog. In our case, one of the potential audits was mandatory to cover the risk area in another quarter. For the three unscheduled risk-based audits, we could cover these in the next quarter, or we could drop the audit if more urgent risks come to light in the meantime. Everything we do in the agile process is a balancing of risk to resources. Again, the audits or special projects we are not taking on now become our future audit backlog.

Take note that each round of audits starts and ends together. In this process, the design is to have the audits operating on a set cadence with a predictable flow of insights released to management. One of our primary goals is to provide insights to management more quickly. This example can produce senior management insights every six weeks, or every quarter, depending on your organization. A future maturity goal would be to produce insights on demand.

Table 5.3 Example Agile Audit schedule with sprints

	SPRINT 1		SPRINT 2		SPRINT 3		SPRINT 1		SPRINT 2		SPRINT 3	
	WEEK 1	WEEK 2	WEEK 3	WEEK 4	WEEK 5	WEEK 6	WEEK 7	WEEK 8	WEEK 9	WEEK 10	WEEK 11	WEEK 12
Team 1	Employee Safety at Work (845 hours)						Product Environmental Safety (845 hours)					
Oliver	195 hours						195 hours					
Steven	208 hours						208 hours					
Tamika	208 hours						208 hours					
Jayden	234 hours						234 hours					
Team 2	Talent Acquisition (871 hours)						SOX Audit (871 hours)					
Tom	195 hours						195 hours					
Robinson	208 hours						416 hours					
Jackson	234 hours						234 hours					
Jasmine	234 hours						234 hours					
Team 3	Equipment Acquisition (845 hours)						GDPR Audit (845 hours)					
Tess	195 hours						195 hours					
Jennifer	208 hours						208 hours					
Leila	208 hours						208 hours					
Laura	234 hours						234 hours					

Key | Manager | Senior | Staff

Team Member Selection

The agile audit teams should ideally stay together across multiple audits. Continuity allows the team to develop better a cohesive group, and it facilitates the ability to end audits sooner and pull forward the next audit. Team design will often depend on the mix of skills needed to complete the types of audits in your specific organization. As a best practice, many successful teams are designed with a diversity of thought in mind. This design allows the team flexibility to take on a variety of topics.

Including SMEs

Teams will not always have the perfect resource mix or the skills needed for every test. Subject matter experts (SMEs) should be used to augment the team's skills set. Today, SMEs may have specific audit skills like data analytics, data mining, or technical accounting. They may also come from outside of audit. Borrowing a SME from within your organization or hiring an outside consultant can be extremely helpful when auditing an unfamiliar area. SMEs can supplement the team for the entire audit, sprint, or even a single test.

With everything we have covered in this chapter, we can now visualize the agile audit process as depicted in the model below. The planning process in the audit lifecycle produces an audit backlog that replaces the traditional audit plan.

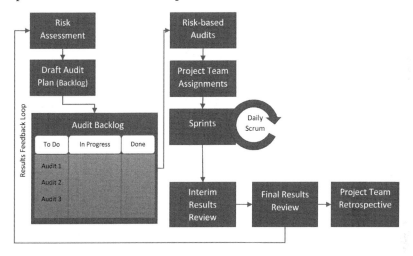

Figure 5.1 Agile Audit process from assessment to retrospective

Discussion Questions

- What are your organization's strategic goals and objectives?
- Who in your organization will you involve in discussions about emerging risks? Consider senior management, risk management, compliance, and other assurance teams.
- How mature is your data analytics program?
- Have you considered exploratory testing before?
- Do you believe your current planning process is risk-based? Why or why not?
- Can you tie your audit plan back to organizational objectives?

- What is your department's mix of mandatory and risk-based audits?
- Do you feel this mix is appropriate, or do you believe your plan should include more risk-based audits?
- How long are your audit projects?
- What causes your audits to extend beyond the expected end date?

Case Study

Gabi and the directors, Mike and Pam, were able to build the audit plan very quickly. This was the fastest planning session they had held in years. The teams were already set, and the risk prioritization effort made choosing the audits as simple as going down the list in order.

To finalize the planning effort, the teams were plotted into a calendar to set the timeboxes. Three teams would complete six audits (two projects each) for the first quarter of the year. Mike and Pam would serve as scrum masters on the projects. Mike would act as scrum master for Team 1 and Team 2, while Pam would take on Team 3.

Table 5.4 Example Agile Audit schedule

	SPRINT 1		SPRINT 2		SPRINT 3		SPRINT 1		SPRINT 2		SPRINT 3	
	WEEK 1	WEEK 2	WEEK 3	WEEK 4	WEEK 5	WEEK 6	WEEK 7	WEEK 8	WEEK 9	WEEK 10	WEEK 11	WEEK 12
Team 1												
Mike	Employee Safety at Work (845 hours)						Product Environmental Safety (845 hours)					
Oliver	195 hours						195 hours					
Steven	208 hours						208 hours					
Tamika	208 hours						208 hours					
Jayden	234 hours						234 hours					
Team 2												
Mike	Talent Acquisition (871 hours)						SOX Audit (871 hours)					
Tom	195 hours						195 hours					
Robinson	208 hours						416 hours					
Jackson	234 hours						234 hours					
Jasmine	234 hours						234 hours					
Team 3												
Pam	Equipment Acquisition (845 hours)						GDPR Audit (845 hours)					
Tess	195 hours						195 hours					
Jennifer	208 hours						208 hours					
Leila	208 hours						208 hours					
Laura	234 hours						234 hours					

Key	Manager	Senior	Staff

Before starting fieldwork, Avery was engaged to provide scrum master training for Mike and Pam. The training program was designed to address the following areas:

- Acting as a servant leader and the voice of the audit team
- Coaching team improvement with values, principles, and best practices
- Enabling close cooperation across all roles within the cross-functional team
- Assisting Gabi in preparing and refining the backlog
- Protecting the team from external influence
- Supporting the team rules (Work in Process limits)
- Facilitating the team's progress toward team goals
- Leading team efforts in process improvement
- Facilitating events – (Daily Stand-up, Planning, Review, and Retrospective)
- Eliminating roadblocks
- Promoting quality best practices
- Building a high-performing team
- Coordinating with other teams
- Supporting agile adoption
- Facilitating board report creation

In addition to the training, Avery plans to provide hands-on guidance to Mike and Pam for the first two weeks of the audit. Avery will perform the first few daily scrum meetings and then observe as they take over the meetings themselves. With the training completed and the plan for the mentoring set, the team decided it was time to start fieldwork.

Gabi started the audit execution process by sending out engagement letters for the first three projects. Since she was trying to get ahead of the issues experienced in the past, Gabi included verbiage in the letters to address the risks. Here is one of the letters:

Internal Audit Engagement Notice

Date: February 27, 20xx

To Whom It May Concern:

Internal Audit will be performing an audit of the risks related to workplace safety. The audit will start on April 2, 20xx, and end on or before May 11, 20xx. To achieve the objective of evaluating the organization's ability to protect our employees, the audit scope will cover all controls related to mitigating workplace safety risks.

To assist us with this audit, we would like to obtain some documentation before fieldwork. Please provide the following documentation:

- Safety policies and procedures
- Safety training and effectiveness evaluation
- Accident reports from the past year
- Worker's compensation claims from the past year
- Employee attendance records for the past year compared to PTO and company holidays1

Since we employ an agile audit process, we will need documentation within one week. Subsequent requests will also need to be returned within three days if possible.

We require you to designate a key member of your staff who will attend our daily scrum meetings. Sprint review meetings will occur every two weeks to review the audit's progress, roadblocks, and issues. The final sprint review will serve as the audit closing meeting. Action plans for any issues found will be set at that point, and only a single-page executive summary report will be published. Issues will move directly into the remediation phase.

We look forward to working with you and your team in the coming weeks. If you have any questions, please reach out to Mike or me directly. The team will introduce themselves during the kickoff meeting on Monday afternoon. We have already made meeting arrangements with your administrative assistant.

Thanks in advance,

Gabi, Chief Audit Executive

6

AGILE AUDIT EXECUTION

Now that we have an audit plan, we move into the execution, or field-work, phase. We can apply an agile, risk-based approach to ensure the most critical areas are given the highest priority within fieldwork.

Organizing the Audit

In agile terms, an audit is a story, and each risk is a sprint. We perform an audit to understand a topic well enough to tell senior management a story about what the organization is doing well or needs to improve. In a sprint, we define the scope of work to complete and plan our approach. Likewise, we define the risk and controls' scope to test, dividing the testing among team members. At the end of each sprint, we will include a results review meeting with management to review the uncovered issues.

Managing the Audit Engagement

The details of testing in an agile environment are the same as any traditional method. The most significant difference is in project management. We will employ various agile tools and techniques to accomplish our goal of auditing the highest priority risks and completing the project on time.

Scrum Board

While there are many methods, the most common agile management tool is a scrum board. A scrum board visualizes the stages for managing the audit engagement. The stage names are up to you, but these should capture the same meaning as the list below. The scrum board has five or six columns (see below):

- Audit (Story in Agile)
- To Do

DOI: 10.1201/9781003201571-6

- Blocked (optional)
- In Progress
- In Review
- Done

Figure 6.1   Example of an Audit Plan Scrum Board

Depending on the board you design, you can need to identify the audit. If you only include one audit per board, eliminate this column and include the audit name in the board title below. You will only need the column if you include multiple projects on a single board.

Figure 6.2   Example of an Audit Project Scrum Board

The next column is "To Do." The column captures the risks that still need testing. At the start of the audit, the column includes all the risks in scope for the audit.

You can include an optional column next to capture any testing that is currently blocked. As testing begins, auditees may slow the work by holding up documentation requests or not providing interview time. Items in this column have moved backward from the subsequent "In Progress" column.

The "In Progress" column holds all items the team is currently testing in the audit. The goal is to complete each item within one to two weeks. As you complete testing, the risk moves to the review column. If the work stalls, it moves the Blocked column.

Once the auditors complete testing, the work moves to an "In Review" column. Now the audit lead or manager takes on the review process. The item should remain in the column while the lead reviews the test, adds updates, verifies issues, and finally moves to the "Done" column. Tests with issues should remain in this status until the team shares the identified issues with the auditee.

The "Done" column signifies that the work on the risk is complete. Unless new information comes up during testing, the items in the final column should remain completed. The Definition of Done usually indicates that the testing has been completed, supported, and reviewed, with all issues communicated to the auditee. Once all risks and administrative tasks are in the final column, the audit is complete.

Burn-Down Chart

Another useful audit management tool is the burn-down chart. A burn-down chart is a graphical representation of work left to do versus time. Burn-down charts are a run chart of outstanding work compared to the goal timeline. The outstanding work is often on the vertical axis, with time along the horizontal.

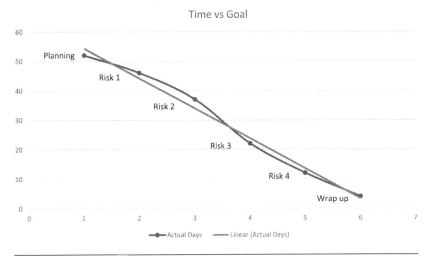

Figure 6.3 Example of a Burn-Down Chart

Definition of Done

One of the benefits we strive to achieve is to eliminate scope creep in executing an agile audit. One way to eliminate scoop creep is through the definition of done. Our traditional audits tended to lack any finality in scope. We typically ended the audit based on completing an arbitrary audit program. Since the agile method is developed based on specific risks and associated controls, we declare the work finished when we have tested the key controls associated with risk.

Retrospective

An important element of the agile mindset is continuous improvement. The retrospective aims to facilitate an open, organized discussion about the project to make process improvements. The format is the same as was described in the section *"Audit Engagement Reporting."* We organize the retrospective into four sections:

Project Review - Review the project facts: goals, timeline, budget, major events, and success metrics, and create a shared pool of information to help everyone remember the details.

What Worked – Ensure everyone shares what they learned during the project. The goal is to understand the reason behind the success and acknowledge all the good things.

What to Improve - Unearth difficulties, issues, and dissatisfactions that the team is currently facing. Do not assess the performance of any individual or penalize anyone; just keep the dialog flowing.

Action Planning - Real change is the ultimate measure of a retrospective's success. End the meeting by creating a specific action plan for improvements. Action plans should be concrete with owners and implementation dates. Brainstorm ideas for future innovation.

Auditing in Sprints

In the traditional method, each person takes their audit programs or control objectives and sets off until the end of the audit to get their work done. In an agile audit execution process, we have two choices. Either we can change our methodology so that the team would all work on one risk until completing the work, or we can assign risks to each person. In either case, we complete agile audit execution based on the ranked risks, prioritizing the highest risks in the audit plan, and addressing these first during fieldwork. Then we subdivide the risk into controls and related tests into sprints. Generally, audit sprints last one or two weeks. After addressing the first risk, we divide the next risk among the team. By completing the work this way, we tackle the highest priority risks in order of assessed ranking.

Daily Standup Meetings

In the agile audit, we replace occasional status update meetings with daily standup meetings. Daily standup (or daily scrum) meetings are important to the success of the audit. The audit team requires open, frequent communication to keep the test work on track, overcome roadblocks, and ultimately complete the audit. These meetings should be short and to the point. The meeting can also include key individuals from the auditee. You may find the auditee is not always willing to come to a daily meeting, but you should encourage them to attend at least every week.

Since we are working within a specific time frame or a time box, we must complete the work on the last day of the audit. We have no room for scope creep, delays, or wasted effort, so we complete the audit as planned, in a prioritized, risk-based approach.

Historically, we have four roadblocks to complete a project on time:

- Delays in getting supporting documentation
- Scope creep, sometimes due to expanded testing
- Reviewing at the end of the audit
- Arguing over the audit report

When planning an agile audit, we will establish several expectations with management to address these common roadblocks before the audit. In the engagement letter, we are already documenting the scope and objectives of the audit. We should also include expectations for the execution of the audit. Explain in the letter that we will provide an initial documentation request on the first day of the audit (or sooner) and need the documents by a specific date. Also, set the expectation that we anticipate subsequent requests, and we would like these returned within three days from the request if possible. By setting the expectation up front, we can escalate delays when needed.

We are familiar with documenting the audit scope, but we often keep the terms vague to allow us some room to maneuver if required. To avoid scope creep, we should define the scope as accurately as possible. We now define the audit according to risk terms, and starting with risks can be a dramatic shift. We can take a real-world example to understand what this means.

For example, in a traditional Human Resources audit, we focus on the end-to-end hiring process, paperwork compliance, onboarding, pay, evaluations, promotions, and terminations. We could spend weeks looking through filing cabinets and validating as much as we are able. In an agile audit, we focus on the highest, most pressing risks related to Human Resources. The risks would be, as an example, discrimination in hiring practices, wage disparity among genders or races, or unsafe working conditions. We are setting up an extremely different audit when we focus on risk, and we are unlikely to crack open a filing cabinet ever during the agile audit. That's not to say that traditional compliance and process reviews are not important, but it is not the focus of an agile audit.

The next common roadblock is the review process. In this case, the issue is often within our habits. We need a mechanism/technology solution for documenting work, signing off on the work, and evidencing our review. The auditors in the field must be diligent about completing the work on time, and the review needs to happen as near to real-time as possible. A real-time review is the only way to have adequate time to identify and confirm issues to report to management.

The last roadblock is arguing over the audit report. As with the other blocks, we should set expectations before the start of the audit. The agile audit process requires open communication between the audit team and those involved in the audit. We complete the work in short sprints (one to two weeks), so we plan for a meeting at the end of each sprint to discuss the current finding and develop a plan to address these in that meeting. We will discuss more on the reporting aspects of the agile audit in the next section.

The team will discuss each of these roadblocks during the daily standup meetings. At the start of the audit, we set the expectations and invite the auditee to the daily event to prevent work blockage.

Managing the Audit Team

The scrum master trusts the agile audit team to get the work done. Once the initial plan is implemented, completing the audit means testing the relevant controls associated with the prioritized risks. The scrum master keeps the team on track by ensuring the testing is completed before the team members move on and keeping track of which team member is working on each risk. So, the team can move through the risks on their own as they complete testing.

Sprint Reviews with Management

One of the ideas in an agile environment is to have a deliverable product at the end of each sprint. The product we as auditors produce is insights into risks for management. Agile audits end each sprint with a sprint review to communicate issues and acknowledge successes with the auditee. Some agile audit departments will produce a formal audit report at the end of each sprint. The Standards NEVER actually required us to write an audit report. The requirement is to communicate scope, objectives, and results (see Standard 2410 below). Likewise, the sprint review's goal is to communicate the prior week's testing results effectively and efficiently.

We organize the meeting into four steps, and the entire meeting lasts just 30 minutes. The four steps should be written on a whiteboard, projected in a room, or otherwise shared via web conference for everyone to see. Here are the steps:

Step 1.   Set the stage. (5 min)
Step 2.   What went well? (10 min)
Step 3.   What needs improvement? (10 min)
Step 4.   Next steps (5 min)

In Step 1, we start by reviewing the prior week's scope. The scope should include the risks and associated controls we tested. Step 2 is acknowledging the audit areas that went well and documenting these areas. Talking about what went well will feel like a foreign concept for some auditors since not everyone includes positive feedback in traditional audit reports. (Refer to Standard 2410.A2.)

2410 – Criteria for Communicating - Communications must include the engagement's objectives, scope, and results.

- 2410.A1 – Final communication of engagement results must include applicable conclusions, as well as applicable recommendations and/or action plans. Where appropriate, the internal auditors' opinion should be provided.
- 2410.A2 – Internal auditors are encouraged to acknowledge satisfactory performance in engagement communications.

The next two steps are related to issues and action plans. In Step 3, we share the issues we found. Remember to follow issue writing best practices. By including the criteria, condition, cause, and effect on the issue, we are less likely to experience management resistance.

Below is an example of a well-written issue:

Issue: Lack of water safety equipment on collection vehicles.

Criteria: All watercraft used in collecting sea plastics must have appropriate safety equipment, including floatation devices and emergency flares.

Condition: In our review of the collection vehicles, we found that floatation devices were too large to fit all employees.

Cause: Watercraft used in the collection of sea plastics is equipped with basic (one-size-fits-all) life vests only.

Effect: Poorly fitting life vests increase the risk of injury or death in an emergency.

Recommendation: We recommend diversifying the onboard safety equipment sizes or providing an expense reimbursement to employees who can purchase an appropriate personal life vest.

Action Plan: Employees on collection vehicles will be provided an approved life vest. Each employee will be allowed to select a branded life vest in the proper size from an intranet site. Personal life vests will be provided within one week.

Owner: James Reagan, Collection Safety Coordinator.

Expected Remediation Date: June 1, 20xx.

In Step 4, we cover the next steps, which in this case, means agreeing to corrective action plans.

After finding an issue, we spend too much time documenting the issue for the report's purpose in our traditional process. When the original reason for the report was as a communication aid, it's clear we have lost the true meaning of the report. We spend too much time wordsmithing, arguing over language, and waiting for formal written responses. When we are agile, issue follow-up can start immediately after the retrospective meeting. If you choose to create any reports to share issue information with others, such as legal counsel or external auditors, this is completely up to you and your organization.

Discussion Questions

How do you think a scrum board and burn-down chart would work in your environment?

What tools do you currently have for managing audit progress?

Considering your department's current tracking processes, do you have consistency across all your audits and audit managers?

How long are your audit projects?

How much time do you spend on the audit report? What value do you see from the formality of the written audit report? Are you open to changing this process?

What causes your audits to extend beyond the expected end date? How often do your audits extend beyond the expected end date?

Do you currently have a formal meeting with your auditees weekly to discuss audit progress and issues found?

What other roadblocks have you experienced? How did you work through these blocks?

Do you think the auditees will attend the daily standup meetings?

Case Study

On the first day of the audit sprint, Avery led the scrum meeting. He started by asking if anything in the audit scope the team needed more information to understand. Next, he asked each team member if they had enough documentation to get started. Since it was the first day, everyone knew that more documentation would come from management soon. The team planned to start the day with documentation review and scheduling interviews.

The next morning, Avery again led the sprint meeting. He asked if there were any problems getting interviews. One person said that they had received an "out-of-office" auto-reply, and they did not know who else to ask. Avery said he would find out and asked the person to continue with the document review.

Avery and Mike then went to their contact within the auditee's organization. They explained the situation and asked whom they should reach out to get an interview on the subject. The contact found the individual's director, who was available and knowledgeable about the area. They set the interview for that afternoon.

On the third day, Mike led the scrum meeting. He started by asking how everyone's evening had gone, asked for a status update on the work so far, and then told everyone about the success of getting the interview the day before. Finally, Mike asked if there was anything that he could do to help keep things moving. No one spoke up, so he ended the scrum meeting.

Avery pulled Mike aside after the team had left. He asked, "Mike, how do you think that scrum meeting went?"

"I think it was fine," Mike said. "It seems like everything is still moving along."

"Let me ask you, Mike. Is anyone having trouble getting interviews scheduled or getting documentation?" asked Avery.

"I assume they are not," said Mike. "No one spoke up."

Avery explained, "We can never make assumptions in an agile environment. While treating a scrum like a traditional meeting is tempting, the scrum meeting has a specific purpose to the scrum master. The scrum is your time to uncover roadblocks. You don't need to open with pleasantries, and it's not the time for a status update. We can handle status through real-time dashboards directly from the audit documentation tool and follow-up emails. To get the most out of the time, ask directly about the items you know the team needs. For now, at the start of the audit, that's interview and documents."

"I see," said Mike. "I guess I'm so used to the old way it was easy to slip back in my old routine. I thought your meeting yesterday was a bit too blunt, and I wanted to make it friendly."

"I get that," said Avery. "There is nothing wrong with keeping it friendly, but remember these scrum meetings will happen every day. In the long run, the team will appreciate you keeping the meeting short and to the point."

7

AGILE AUDIT REPORTING

Agile audit reporting encompasses two types of reports: audit engagement and audit committee reports. As we explained in Chapter 6, audit engagement reports are not required to meet the IIA Standards, but many departments still choose to produce the report.

Audit Engagement Reporting

If we follow the concepts discussed in the sprint reviews, the end of the audit should be non-climactic. The final sprint review is the closing meeting. All the issues were discussed with management as these were found, so the closing meeting only covers the issues found in the final sprint. At the end of the audit, we can prepare a report if needed for communication purposes. For those organizations required to produce reports for public dissemination, it may be helpful to consider the nature of those reports. Producing wordy reports often hurts the transmission of information. If you need to produce a senior management report, the report should contain more summary information and be visual in nature.

> Providing insight into the risk and control environment with senior leadership is the final measure of success.

Any report we produce should communicate a specific message to the intended audience. The traditional audit report is often designed to meet the IIA Standards explicitly. The result is a report full of audit jargon that distorts the message. To illustrate the need to replace jargon with common terms, we can examine the words we use in the audit report. The audit report is a customer-facing document produced by the audit team, but we do not always consider the audience when we write the report. Senior management may be fine with audit jargon after years of exposure, but we also report to the team we audited. They may, in turn, share the report with their staff or with the public in some cases. The table below provides a comparison of common audit jargon to possible terms we could use as replacements.

Table 7.1 Examples of audit jargon

AUDIT JARGON EXAMPLES	POSSIBLE REPLACEMENT TERMS
Scope	What We Reviewed
Objective	Why Did We Perform the Review
Issues/Findings/Observations	What We Found
Criteria	What We Looked For
Condition	What We Observed
Cause	How It Happened
Effect	Why It Matters

In an agile audit environment, we need to design our audit processes to prevent roadblocks from occurring. Since we know that both drafting and arguing over the audit report are major roadblocks to complete the audit on time, we can control this risk by designing reporting that meets our needs, communicates the message, and avoids confrontation.

One effective method is to create a single-page infographic instead of a multipage report. Since the scope of an agile review is often defined as a small grouping of risks, or even just one risk, the nature of the audit is more conducive to infographic reporting.

Audit Committee Reporting

The typical audit committee relationship includes quarterly reporting. If you are not holding quarterly meetings, this will likely be your goal. Ultimately, our goal is to facilitate real-time, on-demand reporting. If you remember from the section on audit planning, we intentionally designed the audits to end on a set cadence. By organizing the work this way, we can end all the audit sprints simultaneously, deliver the results simultaneously, and end the audits together.

> Deliver audit insights frequently, with real-time results during an audit and at least quarterly to the audit committee, with a preference for the shorter timescale

The results we provide to the audit committee must provide insight into the organization's risk and control environment. Too many traditional audit committee reports include countless slides with endless statistics.

Audit Results Visualization

The audit committee meeting's primary purpose is to update the controls related to the risks that could impede the organization from meeting the strategic objective. The reporting should contain visual representations that focus on risks, the control environment, and issues trending by categorizations. In an audit engagement report, the issues should include charts and visualizations that help the reader understand the nature and impact of the risk exposure the issue represents.

Reporting Within the Timebox

By far, one of the most time-consuming aspects of a traditional internal audit activity is the audit report. Many departments spend several weeks or more editing, negotiating language, and sanitizing each issue's tone, that the audit's impact has passed, and the meaning of each issue is lost. When the report is issued, much of the concern is caused by fear. The auditee fears damage to their reputation and possible retaliation for the issues. Auditors fear the confrontation that will come from the report. This fear can be alleviated by changing the format from a lengthy written report to a presentation format. When the focus shifts to discussing the issues openly and finding a solution, fear is reduced. Changing the deliverable from a long-form report to an infographic with an executive summary dramatically impacts the tone of the conversation.

Agile Audit Committee Frequency

The internal audit team is the eyes and ears of the audit committee. As such, the audit committee needs information quickly. For most organizations, the CAE updates the audit committee once each quarter. In an agile team, the frequency should be increased. The goal is to report information as close to real-time as possible. When the audit sprints are aligned, the results are presented to the auditees at the end of each quarter. The team can compile the results and feed the data to the audit committee.

Agile Audit Committee Format

The format of the audit committee report is just as important as increasing the format. To achieve real-time reporting, the use of technology is critical. The issues should be aggregated and presented in an easily digestible visual format. Now that the audit committee has access to real-time information in the same format they would see in a meeting, the CAE can spend the actual meeting time discussing trends, risk exposure, and finally, the state of the audit department.

Presentation Development

The presentation itself can also change. Developing the presentation is another time-consuming drain on the audit department. The key to reducing effort for the audit committee meeting is automation. The data can be fed into software for analysis and presentation directly from the audit results. If automation is not an option, the presentation should focus on trends and risk exposure using clean visuals.

Discussion Questions

How satisfied are you with your current audit reporting process?
What kind of pushback have you received from auditees?
In what ways can you improve the quality of your issue documentation?
What reaction do you anticipate related to a sprint review? Do you think it would be the same across the organization?

Case Study

Audit reporting at Aqua Junk was a nightmare. The audit would end after about six weeks, and the audit report would take another four weeks to complete. Gabi was determined to reduce the amount of time and effort spent on the report. The format she designed highlights the findings but with a positive perspective. For example, in a recent audit, the team found that 10% of the staff did not complete a required safety training. Below is a copy of the full, one-page infographic produced at the end of the audit. To present the issue, the infographic reported that 90% did complete the training with a pie chart showing the result.

Gabi also wanted to ensure the report met the IIA Standards. The standard for reporting is 2410 – Criteria for Communicating that generically requires the team to report on "the engagement's objectives, scope, and results." The standard also says that "results must include applicable conclusions, as well as applicable recommendations and/or action plans."

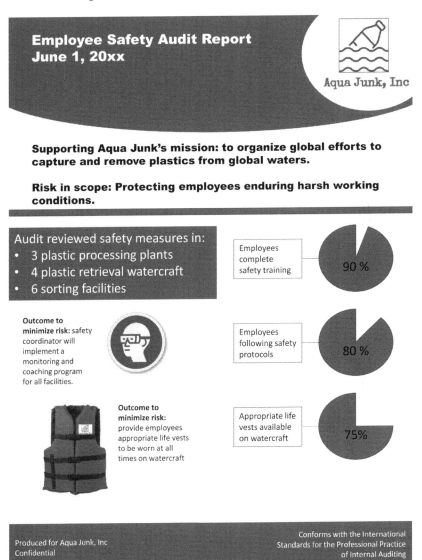

Figure 7.1   Example of an audit report in an infographic format

8

Transition to Agile Audit

With all the groundwork laid in the previous chapters, we now push forward with the transition. The transition itself is a project that will need project management for success. The transition will include planning, piloting audit phases, and adjusting based on the pilot results.

Selling Agile Internally

Auditors usually have a reason for considering a transition to agile audit. For some, there is a push from the organization to adopt the agile mindset. For others, they are leading the charge. In either case, you will probably have to do a bit of marketing for the concept. If you are leading the move to agile, consider how the change will impact your team, your auditees, and the audit committee. If you are part of a larger transition, the focus will primarily be on your team's adoption of the model that works for the audit's purpose.

Establishing Your Agile Transition Objective

When you are building your agile transition plan, the first step is establishing the transition objective. The main question is "What do you hope to achieve with an agile audit transformation?" At the beginning of the process transition, we need to define the extent of the audit lifecycle you intend to move into the agile method. The transition could be a staged transformation or all at once.

When operationalizing your objective, we need to make several key decisions:

- Who will perform tasks?
- How will you organize the team?
- With what length of audit are you comfortable?
- When will the transition occur?

DOI: 10.1201/9781003201571-8

In audit, we have both internal and external stakeholders. Your internal stakeholders will play a part in the audit plan, risk discussions, or broader communication chain. Internally, stakeholders usually include:

- Audit department
- Auditees
- Senior management
- Audit committee
- Audit team
- Assurance partners

Externally, we have responsibilities to the organization as a whole and the organization's customers and business partners. These groups play a peripheral role in the audit department in that they do not directly impact the work we do. They do play into the organization's strategy and strategic risks, which do, in part, drive our audit plan.

Now it's time to enact all the plans made during the transition and make the changes to the areas you have chosen to transition. Not all audit teams transition the full lifecycle. Some teams only make the change to audit execution and plan to change the planning process later. Expect some bumps along the way. As a best practice, set up a short pilot for the processes you plan to transition.

We will plan several important conversations and events during the transition.

- Discussion with the audit committee
- Discussion with the audit department
- Risk discussions with senior management
- Reliance discussions with assurance partners

Each conversation and buy-in from these teams are critical to the transition plan. For example, if we do not have buy-in during a reliance discussion with the risk management team, our transition plan only needs to consider audit coverage.

We need to pick a quarter for the cutover from the traditional method to agile auditing. The shift to agile audit is a major change, so give yourself enough time. With guidance from a consultant, the transition for a typical department may be completed in about 12 weeks, while a larger audit department will take longer.

Building a High Performing Team

Building a high-performing team will allow you to execute the audits with confidence. The team will be able to make decisions during the audit without seeking out managers for approval. To get to this point, you will first need to assess the team's skills. The IIA published a report titled *Core Competencies for Today's Internal Auditor.*[1] In the publication, the skills are organized into two main categories: behavioral skills and technical skills. To truly understand your department's current skill level, you can perform an assessment that rates the individuals across all the skills and the skills across the entire staff. An example assessment is shown below that scores the audit staff horizontally and the skills vertically. The assessment helps you decide how to create a team with a diverse skillset and plan training events for everyone based on skills that need improvement. In the example assessment, each skill is rated on a scale of 1 to 5, with 5 as the highest. Scoring can be gathered through self-assessment, manager assessment, or a combination of both.

Audit Skills Inventory

| Auditor | Behavioral Skills | | | | | | | | | | Technical Skills | | | | | | | | | | Certifications | | | | | | Total Score (0-100) |
	Communication Skills	Interview Skills	Conflict Resolution	Negotiation Skills	Training Skills	Commitment to Learning	Cultural Sensitivity	Organization Skills	Time Management	Accepting Change	Problem Identification	Risk Analysis and Assessment	Control Identification	Testing and Analysis	Audit Standards and Frameworks	Business Acumen	Analytical Skills	Recommending Results and Corrective Actions	Documentation Skills	Facilitation Skills	CIA	CISA	CFE	CRMA	CCSA	CPA	
Macaulay Murphy	4	3	1	1	2	4	4	2	2	2	4	3	1	1	2	4	4	2	2	2	5			5		5	65
Oakley Hurley	3	3	5	1	3	3	4	5	3	2	4	3	3	5	2	4	4	3	2	3	5		5			5	80
Cassius Ahmad	4	3	1	1	2	4	4	2	2	2	3	5	1	1	3	4	3	2	2	2		5	5				61
Asim Wiggins	3	3	3	1	5	4	3	2	2	3	4	3	3	1	2	3	4	2	3	2						5	61
Konnor Snider	4	3	5	3	2	4	4	2	3	2	4	3	5	3	2	4	4	3	2	2	5						69
Loki Copeland	3	1	1	1	2	4	4	5	2	2	4	3	1	5	2	3	4	2	2	3				5	5		64
Can Ritter	3	3	1	1	3	4	4	2	2	2	3	3	1	1	2	3	4	1	2	2	5				5		57
Ellena Summers	4	3	1	5	2	4	4	5	2	2	4	3	1	1	2	4	3	2	3	2	5		5			5	72
Aleyna Ratliff	4	3	5	1	2	4	3	2	2	2	4	5	1	5	2	3	4	2	2	2			5				68
Blade Kline	5	3	1	1	2	4	4	2	3	2	4	3	1	1	2	4	4	2	2	2	5						57
Total	37	28	24	16	25	39	38	29	23	21	38	34	18	24	21	36	38	21	22	22							

Figure 8.1 Example of an Audit Skills Assessment

---

[1] https://na.theiia.org/iiarf/Public%20Documents/Core-Competencies-for-Todays-Internal-Auditor.pdf

In the example above, a third domain for certifications is included. Certifications may be used to encourage longevity in the profession and to demonstrate knowledge. In some cases, certifications also provide a sense of comradery as peers study together for the exams.

Training the Audit Management Team

The audit management team would require the same general skills training as described previously, and they would need training in management/leadership skills. The management skills should include special training in agile methodology to aid the team through the transition. It is common for some audit managers to take on the role of scrum masters within the team. Since they take on this role, they are all expected to receive deeper agile training. The training includes acting as a servant leader and the voice of the agile audit team. They coach the team and facilitate effective agile events. The managers also seek out chances to close gaps across all roles within the cross-functional team. As mentioned before, the main role of the agile scrum master and audit managers is to remove any roadblocks that prevent the team from making progress.

Training the Agile Audit Team

The team training described earlier covered basic audit skills, but there is also a need for agile skills training. The auditors should understand how to define the audit RCM, design tests, and deliver results within the timeboxes of the sprint and project. Many will need to be retrained to see past the audit report as the department's main product. The team will need reminders, especially early on, to provide insights on risk exposure to senior management within the organization.

The agile audit team will need to work together as a cross-functional team, including financial, operational, technical, and compliance auditors with and without data analytical training. They are responsible for planning, executing, and delivering audit work. They all work together to meet the objective of the audit. As a team, they adopt a problem-solving mindset to ensure each risk is evaluated. Under the guidance of a scrum master, they work in harmony, following agile audit practices and organizational policies.

Piloting the Risk Assessment through Planning

Piloting an agile plan should start with the risk assessment. As with the traditional audit process, we need to define the audit universe. Refer to Chapter 4 for a discussion on creating a true risk-based audit universe. Remember, this is a pilot, and it is okay to keep the scope of the redesign small for now. The point of the exercise is to create a proof of concept and test out the ideas you learned earlier.

Once you have the risk assessment completed, choose one or two audits to pilot. With two simultaneous projects running, you will be able to test the teams' ability to work in sync with each other, test the scrum masters' ability to coordinate and reduce the confirmation bias that could result from just one example.

Piloting Audit Execution

For the fieldwork phase of the audit, the scrum master's skills are tested. The team will engage in the kickoff, daily scrums, sprint result meetings, and the retrospective under the guidance of the scrum master. Scrum masters must pay extra attention to the team as there is always a tendency to slip back into old habits and patterns.

Piloting Reporting

The technology resources available to the team will determine how you pilot reporting. If the team already uses audit management or GRC software, you may have the option to release audit results in real-time to management. If you do not have these tools, the pilot may include testing a new report format and issue aggregation for the first time.

Measuring Your Progress

Take an honest assessment of the plan's success. Measure what worked and what did not. Watch for some slippage in the new processes you have implemented. A common area for process creep can be the daily standup. As people move further into the agile audit routine, the meeting often slips into a status update without discussing roadblocks. Make sure the processes stay on track.

Embedding the Mindset

Holding an open discussion with the audit teams after the pilot and following through on their feedback goes a long way in embedding the agile mindset. We can use the same retrospective concepts we learned earlier in our transition. The best news is that you will have successes, so celebrate the wins! Look for early wins along the way. Talk about what went well. Celebrate a successful retrospective in a pilot, celebrate ending an audit on time and budget, celebrate the wins to keep your team encouraged. Change is hard, and the audit team needs to know what they are doing well.

There will be times we do not do such a great job, but it is ok to have failures. We learn from our mistakes, and if we show the team that we truly believe in this philosophy, they will all communicate more openly about their mistakes. With open communication, we can come up with our plan to move forward together.

The Role of Agile Certifications

Since the Agile Manifesto was published, many IT organizations have worked to solidify the basic concepts into a formal structure and understanding. The outcome of these efforts has been used to develop certifications in agile project management.

Project Management Institute

The Project Management Institute (PMI)[2] has developed five agile certifications, with four of these falling under their branding of Discipled Agile:

- PMI Agile Certified Practitioner (PMI-ACP)® Certification
- Disciplined Agile Scrum Master (DASM)™
- Disciplined Agile Senior Scrum Master (DASSM)™
- Disciplined Agile Coach (DAC)™
- Disciplined Agile Value Stream Consultant (DAVSC)™

---

[2] https://www.pmi.org/certifications/agile-certifications

The PMI's approach to agile certifications is to focus on the concept of an agile mindset and highlight the common agile way of working that can be applied to any situation. The certification programs focus on the role you will play in the organization, ranging from a practitioner to scrum master, to coaching.

Scaled Agile

Scaled Agile[3] has developed a series of 14 different certifications based on their proprietary Scaled Agile Framework® (SAFe®). The certifications can be obtained individually, although these do have a progression depending on the role and level of the person working in the agile team. Here are the current options:

- SAFe Agilist Certification
- SAFe Program Consultant Certification
- SAFe Program Consultant Trainer Certification
- SAFe Practitioner Certification
- SAFe Release Train Engineer Certification
- SAFe Scrum Master Certification
- SAFe Advanced Scrum Master Certification
- SAFe DevOps Practitioner Certification
- Agile Product Manager Certification
- Lean Portfolio Manager Certification
- Product Owner/Product Manager Certification
- SAFe Architect Certification
- Agile Software Engineer Certification
- SAFe Government Practitioner Certification

cRiskAcademy

In contrast to the general knowledge options just mentioned, cRiskAcademy[4] and Insight CPE[5] partnered to develop the Certified Agile Auditor Professional (cAAP) certification specifically to meet the internal audit industry's need for more information on implementing

---

[3] https://scaledagile.com/
[4] https://ondemand.criskacademy.com/p/caap/
[5] https://www.insightcpe.com/p/certification

an agile mindset in internal audit. In this certification course, the focus is on practical application of agile principles that include the 4 Agile Audit Values and 12 Agile Audit Principles to transform your department into a high-performing team capable of auditing at the speed of risk. The goal is a blended solution merging internal auditing with agile delivery in a practical approach that you can use immediately.

While certification is not required for you to move into agile auditing, many professionals have it beneficial to pursue one of the basic certifications to ensure they have a solid know base. Of the options available, the most certifications chosen by internal auditors are the:

- Certified Agile Auditor Professional (cAAP)
- SAFe Agilist Certification
- PMI Agile Certified Practitioner (PMI-ACP)® Certification

These three certifications introduce agility and teach you agile mindset. The Certified Agile Auditor Professional (cAAP) is the only one that bridges the gap to include an agile internal audit way of working.

Discussion Questions

What is the driving force behind your transition to agile auditing?

What challenges have you experienced with the traditional audit process?

What do your other stakeholders (e.g., audit committee, senior management, external audit) think of your current process?

What improvements do you envision coming from a transition to agile audit?

How familiar are you with agile project management?

How much research have you completed related to agile auditing?

How would your team react to a full agile methodology update? What about a staged approach?

What might your stakeholders say to dismiss your plan to move to agile? How would you refute their arguments?

When do you think you want to go live with an agile method?

Will you choose a staged approach or a full transition?

How much time do you plan to allocate to the transition?

Do you have a transition team in mind? Whom will you trust
with the task?

Have you researched agile transition consultants?

Case Study

The audit team at Aqua Junk is excited to give agile audit a complete
pilot. Up to this point, they have been making the changes needed to
move their department deeper into the agile mindset. Avery called
the entire team to review the progress made so far and discuss the
pilot plan.

Avery started the meeting with a review of all the work the team
has done during the transition. He pointed out the following bullets
in a presentation in the conference room:

- Rebuilt the audit universe to be risk-based, not entity -based
- Completed the risk assessment with input from new
  sources (management, financial statements, competitor risk
  statements)
- Incorporated emerging risk factors
- Created a 12-week audit plan organized into two-week sprints
- Formed new, cross-functional teams
- Drafted a new engagement letter format with expectation
  setting language
- Met with the audit committee to discuss the new plans
- Formatted a new audit report layout as a single-page
  infographic
- Updated the audit software to facilitate faster audit commit-
  tee reporting
- Held meetings with management to introduce the new pro-
  cesses the team will employ

Gabi joined Avery to thank the team for all the hard work that went
into the transition. And she introduced the pilot. "Even though tested
out the ideas already," she said, "we need to pilot a complete audit
cycle. So, we are going to perform a mini end-to-end pilot."

On the screen, Gabi pulled up two risks. The department would
split into two teams, and each team would take one risk. Each team
will perform an assessment, identify the controls, and develop an

audit plan for that one risk. Then the teams will test the controls over the course of three sprints, each one-week long. Each sprint is to end in a sprint review with management.

"I have already made arrangements with the auditees, and they are prepared for the new approach," Gabi explained. "Oliver and Tom will lead the pilots, with Mike acting as the scrum master. Pam and her team will observe and critique the pilot. We will reconvene in four weeks, but do not hesitate to come to Avery or me for assistance."

With that, the team set off to work through the pilots.

After the pilots were done, the teams were even more excited. Mike and Pam held retrospectives with their teams, and then the entire department came back together for a larger discussion. Avery led a full department retrospective. While the entire pilot was a success, it was not completely perfect. At times, the two teams were trying to book time with the same people for interviews. Also, all the auditors with data analytics skills were on Oliver's team, which slowed down the testing for Tom's team.

On the screen, Avery typed out "coordination between teams" and "cross-functional teams" under the heading "What Needs Improvement." Next, he led a discussion about how they could solve these two concerns on the next round of audits. The team all agreed to the proposed changes, and they called the pilot complete.

9

PLANNING FOR AGILE ASSURANCE

Adopting an agile mindset in internal audit is a big undertaking, but in some respects, it is only the first step toward a larger goal: agile assurance. Agile assurance is a risk-based, iterative approach to assurance, including internal audit, risk management, IT governance, compliance functions, and potentially many other governance functions.

An Agile Audit Maturity Model

Before we bring in other assurance functions, we can take a longer view of internal audit. The nature of an agile mindset leads to continuous improvement. With that in mind, we must plan for growth and maturity. Like most process improvements, implementing agile audit occurs on a maturity curve. We can define three distinct levels of maturity: foundation, sustainable, and expanded.

The foundational stage of the maturity model is primarily focused on transitioning to a quarterly risk assessment and auditing based on risk priority. The sustainable stage encourages cross-functional training and the introduction of analytics into the project's audit planning and fieldwork phases. Finally, the expanded stage is when we begin bringing other assurance functions along the agile path. The model is meant to guide you, not dictate a particular order for achieving maturity. You may have already implemented data analytics on every audit, but you may still create an annual audit plan, so keep this in mind as you consider your current position on the model.

DOI: 10.1201/9781003201571-9

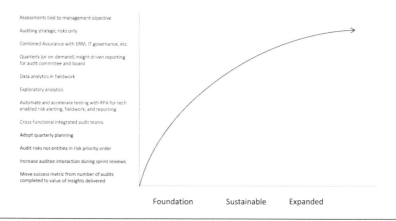

Figure 9.1   Agile Audit Maturity Model

Moving Up the Maturity Model

You can choose to introduce the new method in pieces or all at once. If you choose to take on a full agile audit transformation, it may help to think of the overall change initially as a series of five major process updates:

- Quarterly planning
- Auditing risks
- Agile execution
- Sprint review replacing reports
- Quarterly communication with senior management

Each of these major shifts is part of the larger methodology update we described through this book. After establishing these five foundational elements, we can build on our progress and reach for greater maturity.

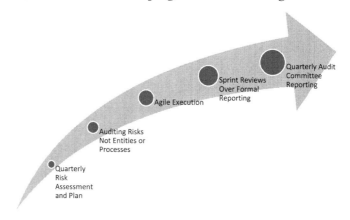

Figure 9.2   Agile Audit Maturity foundational elements

In the sustainable level of maturity, the goal is to deeply embed the agile audit practice into our departments through technology. The way you choose to pursue this sustainability level could include starting a basic analytics program in fieldwork or employing exploratory analytics, as previously discussed. We usually think of data analytics for testing whole populations instead of sampling. Analytics helps us to reorganize data to draw conclusions. Sampling is good for making assumptions about data, but analytics provides actual error rates, highlights trends, and identifies areas for further investigation. More advanced teams might pursue robotic process automation (RPA) for repetitive tasks or establish cross-functional teams with deep domain expertise in technical solutions. RPA automates repetitive tasks by continuously working so auditors can focus on the more dynamic audit work of interviewing, testing, and reporting issues.

By supporting the agile audit process with technology, we increase testing efficiency and automate portions for the agile process to spend our time more effectively performing audit test work.

Planning for Future Growth

You are designing your custom transition to agile audit. You will decide what to take on now and what you would prefer to tackle later during the transition. Again, we are using one of our agile concepts by building our backlog of future enhancements. Keep track of these items.

You could decide to roll out the transition all at once or in stages. It may be better to start with the audit lifecycle's risk assessment and planning phases if you choose stages. Ultimately, the decision is yours.

Recommended stages for agile transformation:

Stage 1: Planning

- Risk assessment
- Audit scheduling
- Backlog development

Stage 2: Audit execution

- Audit plan
- Scoping

- Fieldwork
- Standup meetings
- Retrospective

Stage 3: Reporting

- Audit report
- Audit committee report

The most important advice for anyone transitioning from traditional to agile audit processes is this: do not rush the transition. Remember just how big this change will be for your team. People will be concerned, and they will need reassurance along the way. The best course of action will be to bring in a professional to lead the transformation. A good consultant will work with you to develop a transition plan and then guide you through the plan every step of the way.

The benefits of moving to agile audit are worth the effort. Internal audit has matured from simple compliance to risk-based, and now it's time for us to grow again. As an agile department, we can tactically audit the risks that matter most to our organizations.

Expanding Through Agile Assurance

The third level of maturity expands the reach of agile auditing. The expanded level incorporates cross-department planning to bring other functions like ERM, SOX, IT Governance, EHS, and others all under one objective: supporting management's strategic vision. It would be fair to call our process "agile assurance" at this level since the goal is to bring in other assurance functions, increase collaboration and reliance, and connect all the assurance functions to the organization's strategic objectives.

All the concepts discussed so far still apply when we expand the reach into agile assurance. The focus on coordinating efforts among the Three Lines of Defense has been a common conversation point for several years. Based on the most recent update to IIA Standard 2050, we should consider combining our efforts in audit planning and audit committee reporting in order "to ensure proper coverage and minimize duplication of effort." The responsibility falls on the audit team to review the quality of the work done by other assurance teams and then hold them accountable for their work to rely on them.

We often find overlapping responsibilities among assurance groups within organizations. Internal Audit, Enterprise Risk Management (ERM), and Internal Control, including ICFR/SOX and many other teams, are working toward a common goal to provide assurance and advisory services to management to support the decision-making and risk mitigation processes. Unfortunately, these groups tend to work in silos, which adds to management's assurance fatigue.

Among the many benefits of forming stronger internal partnerships, the assurance functions will adopt a common language when discussing risks, controls, and issues using one consolidated terminology. We will see increased efficiency in collecting and reporting information, and ultimately, we will experience more effective governance, risk, and control (GRC) oversight. Building relevant partnerships with other internal assurance teams will naturally prevent management from being overwhelmed by information and reports and succumbing to assurance fatigue.

In line with our respective audit processes, we should provide more risk information to the audit committee. One way to highlight the current state of our organizational risk profile is with a risk coverage map. In researching the topic, one of the best examples of a risk coverage map in a combined assurance setting comes from a PwC report titled *Implementing a combined assurance approach in the era of King III*.[1] In this report, the authors present the major risk topics for an organization and the groups within the Three Lines of Defense,[2] providing assurance services related to each risk.

---

[1] Implementing a combined assurance approach in the era of King III, *2010* PricewaterhouseCoopers. https://www.pwc.co.za/en/assets/pdf/steeringpoint-kingiii-combined-assurance-11.pdf

[2] IIA Position Paper – The Three Lines of Defense in Effective Risk Management and Control *(2013)* https://na.theiia.org/standards-guidance/Public%20Documents/PP%20The%20Three%20Lines%20of%20Defense%20in%20Effective%20Risk%20Management%20and%20Control.pdf

The example assurance map below from PwC illustrates a combined assurance approach:

Processes assurance assessment

Processes	Three lines of defence assurance providers											
	First line of defence			Second line of defence				Third line of defence				
	Management-based assurance			Risk and legal-based assurance				Independent assurance				
	Control self assessment	Special project	Management review	Risk management	Health and safety	SOX	Compliance	External audit	Internal audit	ISO certification	Consulting engineers	Special project
Strategic												
Cash/finance and treasury												
Funding												
Sustainability												
Growth / mergers & acquisitions												
Alliances												
Operational												
Financial												
IT												
Treasury												
Human resources												
Supply chain management												
Quality												
Environment												
Customers												
Products & services												

Figure 9.3   Example of a combined assurance responsibility map

Suppose we use a risk assessment that includes a comprehensive view of risks identified by all assurance providers in our organization and a combined assurance risk map to show coverage. In that case, we will present management with a more complete and more understandable picture of our organizational risk profile. When building our agile, risk-based audit plan, we are backing our decision with data inputs from the full assurance program. In the end, the risk coverage map serves as both a responsibility chart and demonstrates to management which risks are getting the most attention by all aspects of the organization.

To streamline these teams' efforts and enhance the organizational value of everyone involved, we should consider combining our assurance efforts and aligning our activities, especially in the areas of audit planning and board reporting. Based on the most recent update to the IIA Standards, we have an opening to align our efforts with our assurance partners in order "to ensure proper coverage and minimize duplication of effort" (IIA Standard 2050).

While the idea of relying on the work done by other departments is very attractive, auditors cannot rely on poor quality work, and we typically raise our concerns related to maintaining independence. The IIA has guidance on the topic of reliance. In the Practice Guide *Reliance by Internal Audit on Other Assurance Providers*,[3] the IIA explains the need to assess the other internal assurance provider's objectivity and competence. We can think of this evaluation in much the same way we would a peer review during a Quality Assurance and Improvement Program (QAIP) review.

To ascertain the internal assurance provider's competence, the CAE needs to understand the individuals who make up the other team in much the way we understand our internal audit team.

We must assess the following qualities:

- Education
- Professional experience
- Professional certification
- Policies and procedures
- Supervision
- Documentation standards
- Documentation review
- Performance evaluations

Similarly, the CAE should also decide whether the group can perform the audit work objectively. Considering these groups are generally not independent like an internal audit department, we need to consider the following:

- Who does the assurance provider report to in the organization?
- Will the work performed be influenced by management?
- Are there factors that would prohibit the provider from performing the audit?

For our part in internal audit, we always reserve the right not to use the work performed by our partners, and we can retest or perform our audit of the area if needed. In this way, we do not impair our independence. In the end, internal audit does not report to any of the other assurance teams.

In line with our agile process, we can still deliver quarterly or on-demand audit results to senior management. If we have consolidated

---

[3] Reliance by Internal Audit on Other Assurance Providers, The IIA (2011) https://na.theiia.org/standards-guidance/Member%20Documents/Final%20OAP%20Practice%20Guide%20Dec%202011.pdf

systems across the other assurance providers, then the results can be comprehensive. Some GRC or other audit tools support this level of collaboration. Reaching this level of combined assurance is aspirational, so it may or may not be a goal for your department.

Assessing Audit Maturity

When considering the transition to agile audit, it is good to determine your target maturity level. In the appendix, we have included an assessment tool to gauge where you stand. Use the tools provided as a starting point for your evaluation. Working through this process will sharpen your understanding of why you plan to make this transition and how to communicate with stakeholders.

Embracing Technology Enablement

Throughout the transition process, we have alluded to the use of technology. As you are making your way up the maturity curve, the role of technology increases until becoming an indispensable aspect of your department. For the agile audit and assurance teams, technology can be broken into three groupings:

Generic Tools

Generic tools are all the general use workflow tools, testing tools, agile, and collaboration tools that are sometimes used in internal audit. Many departments use a variety of applications and shared network drives to accomplish their audit work. The main benefit is generally low cost, but these tools are not great for long-term use and even worse for maturity.

Function-Specific Tools

Function-specific tools are applications built for a specific purpose like audit management or SOX tools. Even the broader scope GRC applications usually focus on one aspect of the assurance spectrum for deeper functionality, like risk assessment, and miss the mark on other features.

Assurance Facilitation Tools

Each organization is unique, and there are no perfect technology solutions. The best solution is the one that solves your needs. It may be a single technology or a mix of applications that facilitate your assurance program. As you look for technology solutions, it is important to consider where the functions overlap. Generally, the overlap happens with risk assessment, issue tracking, and reporting. With a shared risk assessment, the entire group can see where the others are covering risks. Issue tracking and reporting should also aggregate data for trends on unmitigated risks.

Anticipating Technology Advancement

Technology never stops, and your technology plan should anticipate growth. The tools you select today will likely be out of date in a few years. Part of embracing technology is embracing its ever-changing nature. Your needs will change as your team matures; and the technology will change as well.

As you move through the maturing phases, your technology needs to advance as well. Here is an example of the technology you may need during the foundation, sustainable, and expanded agile audit and assurance maturity stages.

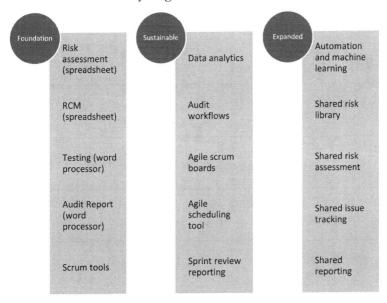

Figure 9.4 Agile Audit Maturity levels with detailed components

Your technology needs may differ, especially if you pull in a more advanced aspect earlier. As a best practice, see what technology is in use in other parts of the organization. You may find that the IT department has access to agile software you may use, or the ERM team may have a risk assessment tool that meets your needs. Often it is easier to expand the use of a current tool than to purchase something new.

Discussion Questions

Have you taken an inventory of the technology and software currently in use within your department?

Do you have an official technology strategy that has been developed to account for growth and advancing maturity?

Has your team had data analytics training on specific applications?

Describe the current relationships between internal audit, risk management, compliance, and other assurance teams?

Case Study

Gabi was excited to share her experiences with others in the organization. For several years, internal audit and the SOX compliance director held meetings twice each year to discuss their respective programs. Since they were closely aligned, Gabi reached out to the SOX director to discuss creating a consolidated risk assessment.

During the meeting, both people shared their risk assessments and upcoming plans. Gabi was surprised to learn that SOX already operated on a quarterly cadence. The SOX director was unaware that the auditors were conducting access reviews of many SOX applications, a control his team also tested.

As Gabi explained the agile audit process her team had implemented, the SOX director had an epiphany. He had been looking for a way to update his team's testing process to follow a risk-based approach. Currently, his team reviews all SOX controls for all processes every quarter. The SOX risk assessment is organized based on ten critical applications, then risks controls. After seeing Gabi's approach, he decided to add a few new score metrics to his current assessment. His updated assessment led to the observation that one application was rated as low risk, four as moderate risk, and five as high risks. Here is an example:

Table 9.1 Example of an Agile SOX testing approach

APPLICATIONS	FINANCIAL MATERIALITY	PROCESS COMPLEXITY	CONTROL OWNER COMPETENCE	CONTROL REVIEWER COMPETENCE	SYSTEM CHANGES	PAST ISSUES	ASSURANCE COVERAGE	TOTAL RISK SCORE
Application 2	High	High	Moderate	High	Low	Low	Low	High
Application 4	High	Low	Moderate	High	High	Low	Moderate	High
Application 7	High	High	Moderate	High	High	Low	Low	High
Application 9	High	High	Moderate	High	Low	Low	Low	High
Application 10	High	High	Low	High	High	High	Moderate	High
Application 1	High	Low	Low	Moderate	Low	Low	Low	Moderate
Application 3	Moderate	High	Moderate	Moderate	Low	High	Moderate	Moderate
Application 5	Low	High	Moderate	Moderate	Low	Low	High	Moderate
Application 8	Moderate	Moderate	Moderate	Moderate	Low	Low	Moderate	Moderate
Application 6	Low	Moderate	Low	High	Low	Low	Moderate	Low

The SOX director decided to change his team's testing approach to test in priority order. Testing for high-risk applications would continue with the current quarterly testing. Moderate risk applications would be tested twice each year, while low-risk applications would be tested once each year.

The testing plan then changed from testing ten applications each quarter to testing based on the priority order of the applications in scope. Here is an example of the test plan.

Table 9.2 Example of an Agile SOX Quarterly plan

Q1 TESTING PLAN	Q2 TESTING PLAN	Q3 TESTING PLAN	Q4 TESTING PLAN
Application 2	Application 4	Application 7	Application 9
Application 1	Application 5	Application 10	Application 5
Application 3	Application 8	Application 1	Application 8
		Application 3	
		Application 6	

After trying out the agile approach to SOX, for a quarter, the director met with Gabi to compare notes and provide an updated plan. He explained that the agile approach had worked better than expected. Many of the challenges the team faced every quarter were lessened with the new way of working and interacting with the control owners.

The team regularly found surprises when testing starts. New technology is regularly introduced into the organization's IT environment without anyone considering if the systems impacted financial reporting. The audit universe in an agile IT SOX audit function starts with a complete application inventory. To keep the listing regularly updated, the team began sending out surveys to the SOX control owners to ask for input on new systems and scheduled upgrades. These systems are now prioritized and assessed for risk ranking by refreshing the risk assessment each quarter. A common issue raised against ITGCs (Information Technology General Controls) is underestimating the scope of a system implementation or upgrade. Having open discussions with management about upcoming changes each quarter provided a perfect opportunity to uncover the scope of a system change and apply either change management or SDLC (System Development Life Cycle) controls.

Since the point of agile is to audit the highest risk areas first, time spent on low-risk applications will be minimized. The volume of testing simply wears out some control owners. The agile approach creates prioritized risk ranking and takes some pressure from the control owners with lower-risk applications.

In addition, the internal audit team was able to review the work done for the critical applications, and they removed these from the possible auditable universe. While the SOX team adopted a different way of working that is not as variable as internal audit, they could better align the programs and eliminate redundant testing. SOX was able to focus its efforts on higher-risk areas and reduce the testing that was not adding value to the company. In the end, the groups committed to quarterly updates and further alignment in the planning sessions.

10
THE WAY FORWARD

Now it is time to answer the main question, "Are you ready to transition to agile auditing?" If you are not sure, take the time to write out the reasons why. This exercise will help you clarify your concerns. If you are ready, then it is time to take the first step.

Taking the First Step

Treat the transition as a project of its own. Since the move to agile audit is a large undertaking, you should manage the project completely. In a large project, the first step is to create a project plan. List out the project objectives, the scope of work, timelines, communication plan, stakeholders, and project risk assessment. Preparing a detailed project plan will help you consider different scenarios to be ready when obstacles appear. See the appendix for an example of an agile audit transformation project plan.

Planning for Mistakes

Somewhere along the way, we lost the ability to learn from our mistakes and carry on. The transition to agile auditing is probably the single biggest change we will undertake in internal audit. The change will impact every phase of the audit life cycle. You will be uncomfortable at times, and you will make mistakes. It is okay to make mistakes if we learn something. Agile auditing has a built-in plan for mistakes. At the end of the pilot phases, you should hold a departmental retrospective. By addressing any issues that came up and all mistakes made, we create an environment of openness and trust within the team. Fixing our mistakes together allows the entire team to learn together at once.

Assessing the Benefits

The final step in the transformation is to decide if the organization will benefit more from a traditional approach or an agile approach to internal audit. In Chapter 1, we discussed the top five benefits that you should expect from agile audit:

- Better alignment to management's expectations
- Deeper insights gained and shared during the audit process
- Increased interaction with auditees throughout the audit lifecycle
- Completing audits on time, on budget, and with higher quality results
- Improved communication within the audit team

Based on the training, piloting, the feedback from auditees and other stakeholders, and the discussions during pilot retrospectives, will this approach provide better information to the organization? Only you can decide.

11
MEETING THE IIA STANDARDS

A common question among internal audit leaders considering a move to agile audit is about compliance with the IIA Standards.[1] The IIA Standards are a consistent set of guidelines used by all internal auditors globally, regardless of industry.

The Standards

The IIA Standards consist of two types of standards: Attribute Standards and Performance Standards. The Attribute Standards address the audit department and function within the organization, while the Performance Standards apply to complete the audit work. The Attribute Standards are not impacted by the move to agile auditing, but many audit leaders still ask about impairment to independence. Standard 1100 – Independence and Objectivity states, "the internal audit activity must be independent, and internal auditors must be objective in performing their work." The question comes up in two areas: the inclusion of the auditee in the daily scrum meeting, and when working toward combined assurance with other internal governance, risk, and control teams.

The Question of Independence

As auditors, we display objectivity and independence, but not everyone can describe what this means. Why is it so difficult? We can develop too much trust in our coworkers. As internal auditors, we are independent and yet still part of an organization. We ride the elevators, have lunch, and volunteer in the community together. The fact

---

[1] https://na.theiia.org/standards-guidance/Public%20Documents/IPPF-Standards-2017.pdf

that we all work together can be a strain on our objectivity. When we make the decision to include the auditee in the daily scrum meeting, they will be more aware of the work we are doing each day. They will also gain deeper insight into the inner workings of the teams and the testing they perform. Having this knowledge is not an impairment. Our independence is impaired when we allow individuals outside of internal audit to sway our judgment or decisions. If a person we have invited to the daily scrum, or any other meeting, were to engage in this type of behavior, they would need to be excluded from the meetings.

The other situation is more complex. Performance Standard 2050 deals with internal and external coordination. There is a predictable progression when we discuss coordination that ranges from simply sharing our plans to relying on the work of others. In sharing plans, we work with the other assurance teams to avoid testing in the same place at the same time. On the other end of the maturity curve, we work directly with other teams and rely on their work being as good as our own, mitigating our need to audit an area they have already reviewed. In the interpretation of this standard provided by the IIA, we read, "A consistent process for the basis of reliance should be established, and the chief audit executive should consider the competency, objectivity, and due professional care of the assurance and consulting service providers." For reliance to work, we must hold the work from other assurance teams to the same standards as our own. They still cannot influence our planning or decision-making process, so we remain independent.

Understanding the Performance Standards

In the table below, we will address the Performance Standards impacted by the move to agile audit. Most of these standards are enhanced by the move to agile auditing while several will have no impact.

Table 11.1   IIA Performance Standards mapped to Agile Audit impact

PERFORMANCE STANDARDS	DETAILS	AGILE AUDIT IMPACT
2000 Managing the internal audit activity	The chief audit executive must effectively manage the internal audit activity to ensure it adds value to the organization.	By focusing the work on the most urgent risks impacting the organization, and delivering insights in real-time to the board, the CAE is adding value.

(Continued)

Table 11.1   IIA Performance Standards mapped to Agile Audit impact   *(Continued)*

PERFORMANCE STANDARDS	DETAILS	AGILE AUDIT IMPACT
2010 Planning	The chief audit executive must establish a risk-based plan to determine the priorities of the internal audit activity, consistent with the organization's goals.	The only real change in planning the audit function is the frequency. By increasing the frequency to quarterly, we shorten the planning horizon and better meet management's expectations.
2020 Communication and approval	The chief audit executive must communicate the internal audit activity's plans and resource requirements, including significant interim changes, to senior management and the board for review and approval. The chief audit executive must also communicate the impact of resource limitations.	Since the move to agile audit is a major shift for the department that will have an impact to how the audits are performed and how internal audit will interact with the organization's stakeholders, this must be discussed with the audit committee. Note that this should be completed very early in the transformation discussion since they may determine that agile audit is not in the best interest of the organization. If you cannot get approval, you should not move forward.
2030 Resource management	The chief audit executive must ensure that internal audit resources are appropriate, sufficient, and effectively deployed to achieve the approved plan.	When you are designing your agile audit teams, you may notice a need for rebalancing skills. For example, if you plan to have a data analytics specialist on every team, this may mean you need to hire or train employees with this skill.
2040 Policy and procedures	The chief audit executive must establish policies and procedures to guide the internal audit activity.	Many departments have an audit manual that explains the team's policies and procedures. During the move into agile audit, the manual should be updated or created if this is missing.
2050 Coordination	The chief audit executive should share information, coordinate activities, and consider relying upon the work of other internal and external assurance and consulting service providers to ensure proper coverage and minimize duplication of efforts.	By working more closely with other assurance functions to prioritize audits based on risk, we can achieve a higher level of coordination. Applying an agile mindset across assurance functions can eliminate the redundant requests for time and documentation from process and control owners. Internal auditors can work closely with the other governance, risk, and control teams to find opportunities to rely on each other when addressing the organization's most urgent risks.

(Continued)

Table 11.1   IIA Performance Standards mapped to Agile Audit impact   *(Continued)*

PERFORMANCE STANDARDS	DETAILS	AGILE AUDIT IMPACT
2060 Reporting to the board of directors	The chief audit executive must report periodically to senior management and the board on the internal audit activity's purpose, authority, responsibility, and performance relative to its plan and on its conformance with the Code of Ethics and the Standards. Reporting must also include significant risk and control issues, including fraud risks, governance issues, and other matters that require the attention of senior management and/or the board.	The set out in agile audit reporting is to reach a level of near real-time reporting or reporting on-demand. While audit results will surely be presented during formal audit committee meetings, there should be an expectation that compiled results are available at any time.
2070 External Service Provider and Organizational Responsibility for Internal Auditing	When an external service provider serves as the internal audit activity, the provider must make the organization aware that the organization has the responsibility for maintaining an effective internal audit activity.	If the internal audit function has been outsourced, the external service provider should decide with the organization which approach, agile or traditional, will provide the results needed by senior management.
2100 Nature of work	The internal audit activity must evaluate and contribute to the improvement of the organization's governance, risk management, and control processes using a systematic, disciplined, and risk-based approach. Internal audit credibility and value are enhanced when auditors are proactive and their evaluations offer new insights and consider future impact.	The nature of audit work in an agile setting is arguably better suited to meet the true meaning behind this standard. The agile audit approach focuses on a highly repeatable risk-based approach that focuses on high priority and emerging risks.

(Continued)

Table 11.1   IIA Performance Standards mapped to Agile Audit impact   *(Continued)*

PERFORMANCE STANDARDS	DETAILS	AGILE AUDIT IMPACT
2110 Governance	The internal audit activity must assess and make appropriate recommendations to improve the organization's governance processes for: Making strategic and operational decisions. Overseeing risk management and control. Promoting appropriate ethics and values within the organization. Ensuring effective organizational performance management and accountability. Communicating risk and control information to appropriate areas of the organization. Coordinating the activities of, and communicating information among, the board, external and internal auditors, other assurance providers, and management.	The strategy behind an agile audit approach is tied directly to the organization's strategic plan. The auditors perform assessments to determine the highest priority risks to achieve the strategic goals and then communicate the results to senior management as soon as possible.
2120 Risk management	The internal audit activity must evaluate the effectiveness and contribute to the improvement of risk management processes.	When the agile audit team performs a risk assessment, the results should be compared to the risk perspective results of the most recent risk management assessment. The two teams will most likely have different approaches and metrics in their assessments, which is expected since the assessments have very different purposes. The audit team will need to evaluate the risk management results for both alignment and to challenge the risk management approach if the results are significantly different.
2130 Control	The internal audit activity must assist the organization in maintaining effective controls by evaluating their effectiveness and efficiency and by promoting continuous improvement.	Within the agile approach, the audits are scoped to cover specific risks and the underlying controls. In this way, the audit team is providing feedback to the organization on the effectiveness and efficiency of the control environment.

(Continued)

Table 11.1   IIA Performance Standards mapped to Agile Audit impact   *(Continued)*

PERFORMANCE STANDARDS	DETAILS	AGILE AUDIT IMPACT
2200 Engagement planning	Internal auditors must develop and document a plan for each engagement, including the engagement's objectives, scope, timing, and resource allocations. The plan must consider the organization's strategies, objectives, and risks relevant to the engagement.	Agile auditing requires specific and detailed plans for each engagement. Since the nature of the agile audit requires the team to identify specific controls, the elements of the engagement will also be detailed. The timing of the audit and asset allocation will be determined based on the engagement and formulated by the scrum master.
2201 Planning considerations	In planning the engagement, internal auditors must consider: The strategies and objectives of the activity being reviewed and the means by which the activity controls its performance. The significant risks to the activity's objectives, resources, and operations and the means by which the potential impact of risk is kept to an acceptable level. The adequacy and effectiveness of the activity's governance, risk management, and control processes compared to a relevant framework or model. The opportunities for making significant improvements to the activity's governance, risk management, and control processes.	The items listed in the planning considerations standard all fall under the purview of the scrum master. Each of these requirements will be addressed during engagement planning.
2210 Engagement objectives	Objectives must be established for each engagement.	The objectives for each audit will be based on the risks in scope for the project.
2220 Engagement scope	The established scope must be sufficient to achieve the objectives of the engagement.	The scope of the engagement will always be the prioritized listing of risks.

(Continued)

Table 11.1 IIA Performance Standards mapped to Agile Audit impact *(Continued)*

PERFORMANCE STANDARDS	DETAILS	AGILE AUDIT IMPACT
2230 Engagement resource allocation	Internal auditors must determine appropriate and sufficient resources to achieve engagement objectives based on an evaluation of the nature and complexity of each engagement, time constraints, and available resources.	Resource allocation is based on skills needed to test controls related to the risks in scope. Since one goal in agile auditing is to maintain a cohesive, multitalented team, we should be prepared for the more common needs to complete the audit. The scrum master is tasked with keeping the engagement on track.
2240 Engagement work program	Internal auditors must develop and document work programs that achieve the engagement objectives.	The work program will be developed to address the risks in scope.
2300 Performing engagement	Internal auditors must identify, analyze, evaluate, and document sufficient information to achieve the engagement's objectives.	Documentation standards do not change in an agile audit team.
2310 Identifying information	Internal auditors must identify sufficient, reliable, relevant, and useful information to achieve the engagement's objectives.	Documentation standards do not change in an agile audit team.
2320 Analysis and evaluation	Internal auditors must base conclusions and engagement results on appropriate analyses and evaluations	Documentation standards do not change in an agile audit team.
2330 Documenting information	Internal auditors must document sufficient, reliable, relevant, and useful information to support the engagement results and conclusions.	Documentation standards do not change in an agile audit team.
2340 Engagement supervision	Engagements must be properly supervised to ensure objectives are achieved, quality is assured, and staff is developed.	The agile audit typically includes more supervision that a traditional audit project. The addition of the scrum master splits the responsibility for supervision into two roles. The scrum master is responsible for keeping the project on track, while the lead or manager is responsible for the quality of the work and staff development.

(Continued)

Table 11.1   IIA Performance Standards mapped to Agile Audit impact   *(Continued)*

PERFORMANCE STANDARDS	DETAILS	AGILE AUDIT IMPACT
2400 Communicating results	Internal auditors must communicate the results of engagements.	Communication is at the heart of agile auditing. The audit team is communicating daily in scrum meetings, the auditee is invited to the daily scrum meetings, sprint reviews are held every one to two weeks, and the results are available for the audit committee faster than in a traditional department that holds results back until the end of the quarter.
2410 Criteria for communicating	Communications must include the engagement's objectives, scope, and results.	Sprint result meetings should be organized to include the objective, scope, results, and even to highlight what went well during the audit.
2420 Quality of communication	Communications must be accurate, objective, clear, concise, constructive, complete, and timely.	Communication quality standards do not change.
2421 Errors and omissions	If a final communication contains a significant error or omission, the chief audit executive must communicate corrected information to all parties who received the original communication.	Errors and omission standards do not change.
2430 Use of "Conducted in Conformance with the International Standards for the Professional Practice of Internal Auditing"	Indicating that engagements are "conducted in conformance with the International Standards for the Professional Practice of Internal Auditing" is appropriate only if supported by the results of the quality assurance and improvement program.	Remaining true to professional practice standards do not change. The scrum master should keep the teams on track to meet the standards.

(Continued)

Table 11.1 IIA Performance Standards mapped to Agile Audit impact *(Continued)*

PERFORMANCE STANDARDS	DETAILS	AGILE AUDIT IMPACT
2431 Engagement disclosure of noncompliance	When nonconformance with the Code of Ethics or the Standards impacts a specific engagement, communication of the results must disclose the: Principle(s) or rule(s) of conduct of the Code of Ethics or the Standard(s) with which full conformance was not achieved. Reason(s) for nonconformance. Impact of nonconformance on the engagement and the communicated engagement results.	Remaining true to professional practice standards do not change. The scrum master should keep the teams on track to meet the standards.
2440 Disseminating results	The chief audit executive must communicate results to the appropriate parties.	The CAE is responsible for communication outside of the department. The results will be compiled for the audit committee, but communication may also be shared with other assurance teams, legal, externals, or regulators.
2450 Overall opinions	When an overall opinion is issued, it must take into account the strategies, objectives, and risks of the organization; and the expectations of senior management, the board, and other stakeholders. The overall opinion must be supported by sufficient, reliable, relevant, and useful information.	Issuing an overall opinion is optional and should be decided by the CAE with input from the audit committee.
2500 Monitoring progress	The chief audit executive must establish and maintain a system to monitor the disposition of results communicated to management.	Issues noted during an audit can be moved into a resolution tracking system after the sprint review.

(Continued)

Table 11.1 IIA Performance Standards mapped to Agile Audit impact *(Continued)*

PERFORMANCE STANDARDS	DETAILS	AGILE AUDIT IMPACT
2600 Communicating the acceptance of risks	When the chief audit executive concludes that management has accepted a level of risk that may be unacceptable to the organization, the chief audit executive must discuss the matter with senior management. If the chief audit executive determines that the matter has not been resolved, the chief audit executive must communicate the matter to the board.	While there is no change in the standard regarding acceptance of risk, the agile approach will generally focus on the highest priority risks to the organization. As such, the level of risk should be mitigated to an acceptable level.

Appendix and Glossary

Audit Maturity Assessment

Choose your response to determine the general maturity of the department. Next, in the assessment key, transfer the response to build your custom transition plan discussion. Remember, there is no right or wrong answer. Your response is the first step on the path to make methodology updates that work for your department.

Question 1: From the following options, choose the response that best describes your reason for exploring agile auditing:
   A. The organization is adopting agile processes as a standard methodology.
   B. The audit committee is pushing for a more responsive risk-based plan.
   C. The audit department is just exploring best practices.
   D. The audit department is seeking a more effective audit methodology.

Question 2: Which of the following statements best describes your audit universe?

A. Our audit universe contains departments or operational locations throughout the organization.

B. Our audit universe is a listing of the audits we have historically completed.

C. Our audit universe is process-based and may cross departmental boundaries.

D. Our universe is a listing of risks that are critical to the organization.

Question 3: How frequently will you update your risk assessment?

A. We complete an annual risk assessment only.

B. We complete an annual risk assessment with minor updates throughout the year.

C. We complete an assessment every six months.

D. We complete an assessment at least every quarter.

Question 4: How often should we update the risk assessment?

A. Never

B. Every two years

C. Annually

D. At least quarterly

Question 5: Which of the following sources will you include in the next risk assessment? Choose all that apply.

A. Input from prior audits

B. Input from senior management

C. Input from financial statements

D. Input on emerging risks

Question 6: How mature is your department's analytics program?

A. Our analytics program is still new

B. Only a few team members are proficient at analytics

C. We use analytics on most audits

D. We use analytics on every audit

Question 7: How long does an agile audit need to last? Refer to the agile audit principles if needed.
  A. Until everyone is happy with the audit report
  B. Until a process has been fully tested
  C. As short as possible
  D. Until we have gained insight into the risk(s) we are auditing

Question 8: What approach should we take when assigning tasks to an audit?.
  A. Assign work just like the last time we did the audit
  B. Assign work based on skills
  C. Assign work based on relationships
  D. Assign work based on risk priority

Question 9: What will be your goal for frequency for auditee involvement in standup meetings?
  A. Only at the end of the audit
  B. Once every two weeks
  C. Once a week
  D. Daily if they are willing

Question 10: What do you think will help most in setting expectations with the auditee?
  A. Sending an email
  B. Sending a traditional engagement letter
  C. Sending an engagement letter and calling the auditee
  D. Formally setting expectations related to requests in the engagement letter

Question 11: How will you communicate audit issues to the auditee?
  A. Sending an email
  B. Issuing an audit report
  C. Conducting a weekly phone call
  D. Holding a weekly retrospective

Question 12: How will you track audit progress?
  A. Tracking however the audit manager chooses
  B. Creating charts in Excel
  C. Using audit management or GRC software
  D. Supplementing existing software with agile tools

Question 13: How will you engage with your internal stakeholders?
  A. Reach out to others as needed
  B. Establish informal relationships
  C. Hold annual assurance meetings
  D. Create formal relationships with quarterly meetings

Audit Maturity Assessment Response Key

Table A.1   Agile Audit Maturity scoring key

QUESTION	EXPERT (4)	ADVANCED (3)	INTERMEDIATE (2)	NOVICE (1)
Question 1	D	C	B	A
Question 2	D	C	B	A
Question 3	D	C	B	A
Question 4	D	C	B	A
Question 5	D	C	B	A
Question 6	D	C	B	A
Question 7	D	C	B	A
Question 8	D	C	B	A
Question 9	D	C	B	A
Question 10	D	C	B	A
Question 11	D	C	B	A
Question 12	D	C	B	A
Question 13	D	C	B	A
Column Total	__/13	__/13	__/13	__/13

Discussion Questions

Which column above has the highest total? The second highest?
Do you agree with the maturity rating? Why or why not?

Articulating Your Agile Audit Maturity Plan

In the maturity assessment, we posed questions to help you think through the reasons for transitioning from traditional audit to agile audit and assess your audit maturity level.

In the form below, copy your responses to each question to build your unique transition plan.

_____

To Internal Audit Stakeholders,

The audit department is transitioning from the traditional audit methodology to agile auditing, because (Response to Question 1) ___ _____. In the current audit process, (Response to Question 2) _____ _____. (Response to Question 3) _____ _____, and we commit to update the risk assessment (Response to Question 4) _____.

In the next risk assessment, we will include (Response to Question 5) _____.

In our testing, we currently (Response to Question 6) _____ _____, and we will strive to increase consistent use of analytics to ensure adequate test coverage. We will also find opportunities to incorporate exploratory analytics into our audit planning process.

As we move into scheduling our audits, we will plan our audits to last (Response to Question 7) _____ _____. We acknowledge the audit should be completed based on risks, so we will (Response to Question 8) _____ _____. To keep the audits on track, we will hold daily meetings to discuss work blocks that include auditee involvement (Response to Question 9) _____.

Since we cannot afford delays in the audit, we will attempt to prevent delays by (Response to Question 10) _____ _____. Expectations about communication will include (Response to Question 11) _____.

Audit projects need to stay on track. To ensure these do not drift, we will track progress by (Response to Question 12) _____ _____. As we move forward, we also want to partner with other internal assurance providers. We will (Response to Question 13) _____ so we can agree on organization-wide coverage on risk testing and coordinate our efforts.

We thank you for your support as we make this crucial transition. If you have any questions or concerns as we move forward on this initiative, please do not hesitate to contact us.

To Internal Audit Stakeholders,

The audit department is transitioning from the traditional audit methodology to agile auditing, because the audit department is seeking a more effective audit methodology. In the current audit process, our universe is a listing of risks that are critical to the organization, and we commit to update the risk assessment at least every quarter.

In the next risk assessment, we will include input from prior audits, input from senior management, input from financial statements, and input on emerging risks.

In our testing, we currently use analytics on most audits, and we will strive to increase consistent use of analytics to ensure adequate test coverage. We will also find opportunities to incorporate exploratory analytics into our audit planning process.

As we move into scheduling our audits, we will plan our audits to last until we have gained insight into the risk(s) we are auditing. We acknowledge the audit should be completed based on risks, so we will assign work based on risk priority. To keep the audits on track, we will hold daily meetings to discuss work blocks that include auditee involvement at least once a week.

Since we cannot afford delays in the audit, we will attempt to prevent delays by formally setting expectations related to requests in the engagement letter. Expectations about communication will include holding a weekly retrospective.

Audit projects need to stay on track. To ensure these do not drift, we will track progress by using our current audit management tool. As we move forward, we also want to partner with other internal assurance providers. We will hold annual assurance meetings and plan to create formal relationships with quarterly meetings in the future so we can agree on organization-wide coverage on risk testing and coordinate our efforts.

We thank you for your support as we make this crucial transition. If you have any questions or concerns as we move forward on this initiative, please do not hesitate to contact us.

Sincerely,

Gabi, Chief Audit Executive

Agile Transformation Example Project Plan

Aqua Junk, Inc

Figure A.1 Example of an Agile Audit transformation project plan

Internal Audit

REVISION HISTORY

DOCUMENT VERSION NUMBER	DOCUMENT REVISION DATE	WRITTEN BY	CHANGE SUMMARY (REFERENCE SECTION[S] CHANGED)
V1.0	xx/xx/xxxx		

DOCUMENT APPROVALS

NAME AND FUNCTION	SIGNATURE	DATE

Project Overview

The internal audit department is transitioning from a traditional approach to planning, executing, and reporting results to an agile audit way of working. The project will include training, coaching, and ultimately the full transition to agile auditing.

Purpose, Scope, and Objectives

The purpose of the change is to better align the internal audit activity with senior leadership's objectives, address the most urgent organizational risks first, and provide insights to management and the board of directors.

We have decided to transform all phases of the audit function, including:

- Risk assessments
- Audit planning
- Audit fieldwork
- Audit reporting
- Issue remediation
- Audit Committee reporting

Service Description

Agile auditing is a customer-centric approach to developing and executing audits, based on a shorter audit lifecycle from assessment to reporting, which focuses on gaining and sharing insights with management related to the most urgent risks in an organization.

Success Factors

Several key success factors will impact the successful transformation to agile audit. These factors must receive full attention from all project team members. The key success factors can be broken down as follows:

- Understanding prioritization
- Alignment with senior leadership objectives
- Embracing the agile mindset
- Committing to long-term change
- Project assumptions
- Planning and analysis

All project team resources will be identified, assigned, and available at the appropriate time of the project.

The Executive Sponsor will keep the project team informed of any company initiatives that might impact this effort so that appropriate and timely action could be taken and decisions made to minimize cost and schedule impact to this project.

Process Readiness

Current processes are documented and ready to be shared with consultants brought in to help with the transformation.

Governance Council

The Governance Council will participate in weekly status meetings with project managers and team leads.

Software Requirements

Currently, we do not anticipate need of new software for this project.

Communication

Communication on progress will be shared between the Chief Audit Executive (CAE) and the Audit Committee Chair. Communication to auditees will occur before the audit start date in the form of the audit announcement letter. The audit team will receive in-person updates each week.

Training

An outside agile audit subject matter expert (SME) will develop training, who will also deliver the training to the audit team.

Agile Audit Pilot

The concepts will be piloted first by phase (i.e., planning, execution, reporting) and then aggregated for an entire audit.

Agile Transition Readiness

Transition readiness will be determined based on the results of the pilot.

Agile Transition Launch

The final transition will be based on the full audit pilot and approval from the audit committee.

Project Risks

Risk is any concern or uncertainty that can adversely affect a project's technical, cost, or schedule performance. While risk is inherent in all projects, risk management minimizes potential negative consequences while enabling appropriate risk-taking associated with innovation.

Risk management applies to the entire process of identifying, analyzing, and mitigating risk.

We will use the following steps to quantify risk factors and record the results where applicable:

- Estimate or calculate the impact and likelihood for each risk
- Prioritize the risks
- Determine mitigation plans
- Identify and manage new risks resulting from the application of corrective action
- Risk Identification

Key project risks will be monitored on-going and discussed at monthly steering committee meetings as needed. Risk identification will be performed regularly throughout the project lifecycle. Risk identification will include both internal and external risks.

All team members are responsible for identifying project risks and communicating them to the Project Manager. The Project Manager will be responsible for documenting the risk and development of the mitigation strategy. The identified risks should be reviewed at the project status meetings. The Project Manager is responsible for assuring appropriate action is taken. If the risk is no longer present, the Project Manager will close out the risk.

Initial risks identified include:

Table A.2   Example of an Agile Audit transformation risk assessment

RISK	LIKELIHOOD	IMPACT	MITIGATION
• Timeline is inaccurate	High	High	Weekly monitoring by the Governance Council
• Cost forecasts are inaccurate	Moderate	Moderate	Weekly monitoring by the Governance Council
• Lack of a change management process (too fast or too slow)	Moderate	Moderate	Timeline is created to meet our specific needs
• Lack of a change control board	Low	Moderate	Governance Council established
• Stakeholders have inaccurate expectations	High	Moderate	Socialization of the solution to stakeholders
• Training isn't available	High	High	Training will be sourced from an SME

(Continued)

Table A.2 Example of an Agile Audit transformation risk assessment *(Continued)*

RISK	LIKELIHOOD	IMPACT	MITIGATION
• Training is inadequate	High	High	Training will be evaluated before the pilot phases
• Lack of commitment from audit managers	Moderate	High	The solution will be presented to the audit manager with a detailed demonstration of an agile audit
• Insufficient internal expertise	Moderate	High	External expertise has been engaged to train internal resources
• The new process fails, and rollback is required	Low	High	A rollback plan in place to minimize disruption

High-Level Schedule (Subject to Change)

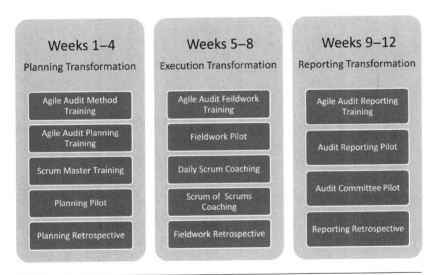

Figure A.2 Agile Audit transformation plan schedule

Project Organizational Structure

The following organizations will participate in this project:

Table A.3 Agile Audit transformation plan roles

COMPANY	TEAM	ROLE
Aqua Junk	Internal Audit	Primary participants in conducting the audit work
	Auditees	Process owners who are the subject of the audit
	Project Management	Project management, business analysis, communication
	Audit Committee	Provides oversight and approval for changes to the audit function
Consultant	Professional Services	SME in agile audit

Project Roles and Responsibilities

Table A.4 Agile Audit transformation plan responsibilities

ROLE	RESPONSIBILITIES
Executive Project Sponsor	Responsible for identifying objectives/strategic direction/vision of the project. Provides linkage to other divisional initiatives. Resolves impasses. Approves work plan, project governance, expenditures, and changes in scope.
Business Project Sponsor	Responsible for overall implementation. Point of contact for implementation team for issues relating to budget, timelines, and overall scope.
Project Manager	Manages the project's day-to-day activities. Conducts weekly updates of the project's detailed plan and budget. Manages project's scope, change control, issues, and acceptance processes. Responsible for overall implementation and execution of the project's governance.
Consultant	Sets the agenda for the transformation based on experience. Responsible for all training and coaching related to the transformation.

Communications Plan

The following table lists the periodic reports:

Table A.5 Agile Audit transformation communications plan

THE REPORT, FREQUENCY, AUTHOR	AUDIENCE	PURPOSE
Project Status Report, Weekly, Project Manager	All members of the audit team	Communicate key information to all team members to ensure awareness and eliminate duplication. Includes a summary of work accomplished during the period, scheduled for the next period, and critical issues.
Executive Status Report, Monthly, Project Manager	All members of the Governance Council	Communicate key information on overall program status vs. objectives and strategic direction. Includes schedule summary, work accomplished, budget vs. plan, and any changes to the original scope, budget, or schedule.

Other critical communication mechanisms include the following:

Table A.6 Agile Audit transformation communication plan for the governance council

ITEM	AUTHOR	AUDIENCE	DESCRIPTION
Change Request	Any team member	Governance Council	Requests a change in scope, budget, or schedule.
Issue	Any team member	Governance Council	An item that is not explicitly in this plan but requires some investigation and effort.
Risk	Any team member	Governance Council	An item that may put the overall project (cost, scope, quality) in jeopardy. As each risk is identified, the assigned investigator will develop a mitigation strategy should the risk occur.

Issue Resolution Process

The following steps will be taken when an issue, risk, or change request (to scope or schedule) is discovered or proposed:

Table A.7   Agile Audit transformation issue resolution plan

TASK	PERFORMED BY
Identify and document issues	Any team member
Assign priority and primary responsibility to generate a proposed resolution for the item	Project Manager
Report progress on item resolution	Project Manager
Monitor and control progress	Governance Council
Communicate proposed resolution	Project Manager/ Implementation Team
Approve or reject the proposed resolution	CAE and Audit Committee Chair

Pilot Plan

Table A.8   Agile Audit transformation pilot plan

TASK	PERFORMED BY
Phase pilots	Team TBD
Issues and changes addressed	Project Manager
Full pilot	Team TBD
Process adjustments	Project Manager

Approval Plan

Table A.9   Agile Audit transformation approval plan

TASK	PERFORMED BY
Go/No Go recommendation	CAE
Go/No Go final approval	Audit Committee

Rollback Contingency Plan

In the event of no approval, the audit team will revert to the traditional way of working while adopting any applicable best practices learned from the experience.

Training Plan

The following table outlines the training plan for this project. Training will be developed and delivered by a third-party Agile Audit SME.

Table A.10 Agile Audit transformation training plan

WHO	AUDIENCE	FORMAT
Agile method overview	Internal audit team	Live, in-person
Scrum master training	Selected scrum masters	Live, in-person
Agile audit fieldwork training	Internal audit team	Live, in-person
Agile audit reporting training	Internal audit team	Live, in-person

Glossary

Agile

Agile is an iterative approach to project management and software development that helps teams deliver value to their customers faster without having to commit to a long project during which time the customer's needs may have changed. An agile team delivers work in small increments more frequently. The main goal in agile is delivering value while responding to change quickly.

Agile Audit

Agile auditing is a customer-centric approach to developing and executing audits, based on a shorter audit lifecycle from assessment to reporting, which focuses on gaining and sharing insights with management related to the most urgent risks in an organization.

Agile Audit Principles

Agile principles were developed to add more detail to the values. Below are the 12 agile audit principles we will follow. These maintain the spirit of the original principles, and each principle in this list is vitally important to the success of an agile audit department.

1. *Our highest priority is to support management's objectives by auditing critical and emerging risks.*
2. *Welcome changing requirements, even while executing the audit plan. Agile auditing accepts change for the best interest of the organization.*
3. *Deliver audit insights frequently, with real-time results during an audit and at least quarterly to the audit committee, with a preference for a shorter timescale.*

4. *Business managers and auditors must work together daily throughout the project.*

5. *Build audits around motivated individuals. Give them the environment and support they need, and trust them to get the job done.*

6. *The most efficient and effective method of conveying information to management and the audit team is face-to-face conversation.*

7. *Providing insight into the risk and control environment with senior leadership is the final measure of progress.*

8. *Agile auditing promotes a timely understanding of risk to operations. The first, second, and third lines of defense should maintain open communication and sharing of results.*

9. *Continuous attention to technical and soft skills enhances audit agility.*

10. *Simplicity – gaining insights into a risk and control environment without expanding the scope – is essential.*

11. *The best assessments, audits, and insights gained emerge from self-managing teams.*

12. *At regular intervals, the team reflects on becoming more effective, then trains and adjusts its processes accordingly.*

Agile Audit Values

The Agile Audit Values are adapted from the Agile Manifesto.

Stakeholder Interactions Over Rigidity and Politics   In any organization, rigid adherence to a communication schedule and influence from internal politics restricts the flow of information from internal audit to management stakeholders who rely on the work done by audit. By placing more value on stakeholder interactions, we increase the flow of information to those who need it.

Insight Delivery Over Formal Reporting   Internal audit provides deep insights into the organization's risk exposure. All too often, the message is diluted or wholly lost as auditees argue with audit management over the verbiage in the audit report. When we focus on delivering insights, the substance of the message takes precedence over the format.

Management Collaboration Over Issue Negotiation   During most audits, control weaknesses will come to light. We should not waste time negotiating through the issue to serve the organization better by collaborating as a team with management. Internal audit has an advantage in that we know whom to involve in interdepartmental corrective actions.

Responding to Risk Over Entity Coverage   Providing insight into organizational risk is the goal of an internal audit. The audit universe, risk assessment, and resulting audit plan must be based on risk and not entities to reach this goal

Agile Manifesto

The Agile Manifesto[1] was drafted in 2001 by software developers who wanted to deliver more value to their customers. The manifesto reads:
   We are uncovering better ways of developing software by doing it and helping others do it.
   Through this work we have come to value:

- ***Individuals and interactions*** *over processes and tools*
- ***Working software*** *over comprehensive documentation*
- ***Customer collaboration*** *over contract negotiation*
- ***Responding to change*** *over following a plan*

That is, while there is value in the items on the right, we value the items on the left more.

Assurance

Assurance is an umbrella term for governance, risk, and control functions within an organization. Assurance teams assure senior management and the board of directors that business operations are working as intended through assessment, testing, and reporting. *See also Combined Assurance.*

Audit

An audit is an evaluation of person or process. Internal auditing is an evaluation of control processes performed by an organization's

---

[1] https://www.agilealliance.org/agile101/the-agile-manifesto/

employees to mitigate the risk of not meeting the organization's stated objectives. Each of the audits listed in the plan should include a well-defined, narrow scope that describes the risks the team will investigate. Audits are the agile equivalent of a story. The point of an agile story is to convey the desired result; therefore, audits should focus on insights to share with senior management.

Audit Committee

The Audit Committee is a subset of the board of directors who oversee internal audit, external audit, and financial reporting. The CAE reports directly to the Audit Committee, not to company management, which establishes the internal audit department's independence.

Audit Committee Reporting

Audit Committee reporting is a periodic, usually quarterly, reporting update on the state of the internal audit department, upcoming audit plans, and risk exposure uncovered during recent audits. Agile auditing seeks to increase the availability of updated information to the Audit Committee to near real-time.

Audit Lead/Scrum Master

The Audit Lead performs a critical role in the audit process. During the audit, the Audit Lead organizes the team to address the risks in scope, conducts the daily standup meeting, facilitates the interim and the final review of results, and reports back to the Audit Plan Owner. In an agile environment, the Audit Lead has several key responsibilities:

- Acts as a servant leader and the voice of the agile audit team
- Coaches team improvement in line with values, principles, and best practices
- Facilitates effective daily standup events, meetings, and retrospectives
- Enables close cooperation across all roles within the cross-functional team

- Assists Audit Plan Owner in preparing and refining the backlog
- Removes roadblocks
- Protects the team from external influence

Audit Objective

The audit objective is a statement of the audit's purpose. The objective should tie directly the organization's strategy.

Audit Plan Owner/Product Owner

The CAE or Audit Director owns primary responsibility for the audit plan. Developing the plan is done in conjunction with senior management. Since the groups are working closely together, the resulting audit plan addresses senior management's most urgent concerns. While not an exhaustive list, the Audit Plan Owner:

- Coordinates with senior management and the board to create and prioritize the audit plan
- Adjusts risks and audit priority continually to enable the delivery of highest value work
- Accepts or rejects work delivered by the team
- Determines insight reporting release cadence based on management's need and opportunity

Audit Program/Sprint

Audit sprints are subsections of an audit. In some cases, the sprints may be made of audit programs or controls. Since we will focus on achieving a genuinely risk-based approach, the ideal sprint will be based on risks to review. Most often, sprints are one to two weeks long, with two-week sprints as the most common.

Audit Project Team/Agile Team

The Audit Project Team is the core of the entire process. The team is designed to explore the risks in scope, evaluate the controls, and determine if any issues need to be communicated back to management. Responsibilities of the team include:

- Agile Audit Team is cross-functional with typically 3–5 people
- Defines, builds, tests, and delivers risk and control testing
- Members are dedicated to the specific value-stream delivery
- Some roles may be shared among multiple teams (e.g., Data Analytics, IT, Compliance)
- Plans for and commits to audit goals for each audit
- Applies quality review practices per IIA Standards
- Participates in agile events to deliver value, gather feedback, and ensure relentless improvement as an Agile Audit Team

Audit Report

The audit report is a communication used as a final output from the audit team on the issues uncovered during the audit. The need for an audit report is derived from the requirement to communicate audit results; however, the report itself is not a requirement, only the communication, which may be achieved in a better format.

Audit Schedule/Timebox

The final audit plan, individual audits, and audit sprints operate within a fixed date range called a timebox. The dates are firm as the entire audit department will operate within synchronized cycles.

Burn-down Chart

While many audit progress reports exist, a burn-down chart is a unique graphical representation of the amount of work left versus the time left within the timebox. Burn-down charts are a run chart of outstanding work compared to the goal timeline. The outstanding work is often on the vertical axis, with time along the horizontal.

Cadence

Cadence is a regular frequency at which an event occurs. Agile auditing should have audit sprints starting and finishing on a set cadence, typically two weeks, so that all audit committee insights are updated at the same time.

Combined Assurance

Combined Assurance is an approach to governance, risk, and control activities in which the different assurance teams collaborate to reduce redundant testing while providing a holistic perspective on the organization's risk response.

Control

A control is a process used to mitigate the impact or likelihood of a risk from preventing the organization from meeting its objectives.

Data Analytics

Data Analytics is the systematic, computer assisted analysis of information. Analytics are used to discover abnormalities, patterns, or other insights in a data set. Analytics are also used for information-based decision-making.

Daily Team Meeting/Daily Scrum/Daily Standup

The meeting includes the audit team and auditees. While a few audit managers already had the practice of daily team meetings, daily standup or daily scrum is a special event. The meeting objective is to discuss progress and roadblocks, not to recap the past.

Definition of Done

The Definition of Done is a formal metric used to determine an audit is complete. Our traditional audits tended to lack any finality in scope. We typically ended the audit based on completing an arbitrary audit program. Since the agile method is developed based on specific risks and associated controls, we declare the work finished when we have tested the key controls associated with risk.

Draft Audit Plan/Backlog

After performing the risk assessment, we developed a list of audits we could perform. At this point, we are not committing to a plan as the backlog includes projects that may or may not end up in the final plan. In a traditional setting, the audit plan is listing of the audits the internal audit department intends to complete over the next one- to three-year horizon. The plan is based on a risk assessment of the organization.

Final Audit Plan/Epic

After prioritizing the draft audit plan, we settle on a final listing of audits we commit to perform within a defined period. An agile audit plan is a prioritized backlog of the risks impacting the organization in the next quarter. The plan is continuous in that the listing of risks is updated based on a quarterly risk assessment that captures new and emerging risks as well as updated prioritization based on input from management and other sources.

GRC

GRC is an acronym for governance, risk, and control. GRC is a function of senior management and the board of directors to maintain control over enterprise risks.

Interim Issue Updates/Sprint Review

At the end of the sprint, the results must be shared with the auditee. These weekly/biweekly meetings recap the scope of work performed in the sprint, what went well, what needs improvement, and action plans. The audit team and the stakeholders attend to review the risks audited and issues found in the current sprint.

Quality Assessment Team/Independent Testing Team

Not all audit departments are large enough to sustain a full professional practice or quality assessment team, but all audit work must be reviewed.

RCM

RCM is an acronym for risk and control matrix. The RCM is typically developed during the planning phase of an audit, and the RCM should include the risks used in the risk assessment as a starting point.

Retrospective

An important element of the agile mindset is continuous improvement. The retrospective aims to facilitate an open, organized discussion about the project to make process improvements. We organize the retrospective into four sections:

  Project Review – Review the project facts: goals, timeline, budget, major events, and success metrics, and create a shared pool of information to help everyone remember the details.

  What Worked – Ensure everyone shares what they learned during the project. The goal is to understand the reason behind the success and acknowledge all the good things.

  What to Improve – Unearth difficulties, issues, and dissatisfactions that the team is currently facing. Do not assess the performance of any individual or penalize anyone; just keep the dialog flowing.

  Action Planning – Real change is the ultimate measure of a retrospective's success. End the meeting by creating a specific action plan for improvements. Action plans should be concrete with owners and implementation dates. Brainstorm ideas for future innovation.

Risk

A risk is an event that prevents the organization from achieving its objectives. The IIA Standards recommend assessing risks based on impact and likelihood.

Risk Assessment

A risk assessment is a systemic approach for reviewing all the relevant risks in the organization.

Risk Management

Risk Management is an assurance team that identifies, assesses, manages, and controls potential events. The Risk Management team informs senior management on the likelihood of achievement of the organization's objectives and potential risk exposure considering the control environment.

Scope

The scope of work is the audit's boundaries. By defining a narrow scope, we control the audit and amount of work assigned to various teams. In agile auditing, the scope can be just one or two risks, unlike complete process audits in the traditional method.

Scrum Board/Kanban Board

While there are many methods, the most common agile management tool is a scrum board. A scrum board visualizes the stages for managing the audit engagement. The stage names are up to you, but these should capture the same meaning as the list below. The scrum board has five or six columns (see below):

- Audit (Story in Agile)
- To Do
- Blocked (optional)
- In Progress
- In Review
- Done

Scrum of Scrums

The scrum master will conduct daily standup meetings and report to the CAE during a scrum of scrums meeting. The scrum of scrums is a gathering of all scrum masters to report to the CAE. The meeting is used to ensure proper communication vertically to the CAE and horizontally to the other scrum masters so there is no duplication of effort.

SMEs

Subject matter experts (SMEs) are those technical and domain experts in the Audit Team with unique skills and knowledge. While we often think of skills such as data analytics, these skills are not isolated to technical skills only. SMEs could be full members of the Agile Project Team or be brought in for specific testing.

SOX

SOX (Sarbanes-Oxley Act of 2002) is a regulatory requirement for public companies in the US to document, test, and certify the effectiveness of their internal controls over financial reporting (ICFR). SOX requirements are sometimes facilitated by the Internal Audit department, sometimes by a dedicated team, but always with management owning the controls. The SOX function is an assurance function.

Sprint/Iteration

A sprint is a one- or two-week iteration of work performed during an audit. We complete agile audit execution based on the ranked risks, prioritizing the highest risks in the audit plan, and addressing these first during fieldwork. Then we subdivide the risk into controls and related tests into sprints. Generally, audit sprints last one or two weeks. After addressing the first risk, we divide the next risk among the team. By completing the work this way, we tackle the highest priority risks in order of assessed ranking.

Sprint Review

The sprint review is a meeting to communicate the prior sprint's testing results effectively and efficiently. We organize the meeting into four steps, and the entire meeting lasts just 30 minutes. The four steps should be written on a whiteboard, projected in a room, or otherwise shared via web conference for everyone to see. Here are the steps:

Step 1.   Set the stage (5 min)
Step 2.   What went well? (10 min)
Step 3.   What needs improvement? (10 min)
Step 4.   Next steps (5 min)

As a best practice, attendance should be limited to decision-makers.

Test

Auditors perform control testing procedures to assess the efficiency and effectiveness of the control processes implemented by management in an organization.

The IIA and the Standards (IPPF)

The IIA (The Institute of Internal Auditors) is the international standard setting organization for all internal auditors. The International Professional Practices Framework (IPPF), generally referred to as the Standards, is "the conceptual framework that organizes authoritative guidance promulgated by The IIA."[2]

Waterfall/Traditional Audit

Waterfall project management has been used in traditional audit planning for many years. In traditional auditing, an audit plan is set for a year with the audit projects created as independent projects. The plan is completed and progress reporting completed each quarter. Each project is also a waterfall that includes planning, testing, review, and reporting.

---

[2] https://na.theiia.org/standards-guidance/Pages/Standards-and-Guidance-IPPF. aspx

Index